Preaching Verse by Verse

Preaching Verse by Verse

Ronald J. Allen
Gilbert L. Bartholomew

Westminster John Knox Press
Louisville, Kentucky

Book design by Sharon Adams
Cover design by Pam Poll

First edition
Published by Westminster John Knox Press
Louisville, Kentucky

This book is printed on acid-free paper that meets the
American National Standards Institute Z39.48 standard. ∞

PRINTED IN THE UNITED STATES OF AMERICA
00 01 02 03 04 05 06 07 08 09 — 10 9 8 7 6 5 4 3 2 1

A catalog card for this book may be obtained
from the Library of Congress

ISBN 0-664-25804-2

CONTENTS

INTRODUCTION

In the last twenty-five years, a revival in homiletics has occurred. Approaches to the sermon have multiplied to the point that the preacher can choose from among a great chorus of homiletical possibilities.[1] Among the most widely known are inductive movement,[2] the sermon as story,[3] the Lowry loop,[4] the sermon as a journey to celebration,[5] the sermon as an act of overhearing,[6] the sermon as a plot of carefully developed moves,[7] the genre and function of the text shaping the genre and function of the sermon,[8] the sermon as an act of the imagination,[9] the sermon as a movement of images,[10] the sermon as a distinctively oral event,[11] the sermon as conversation.[12] The topical sermon is even making a comeback.[13] And blessed are the preachers who create their own homiletical styles.

A preacher derives great benefit from such a large array of approaches. He or she can select or create a homiletical form that serves the needs of a particular sermon to a particular congregation in a particular situation. We can even imagine congregational settings in which the structure of three points and a poem can offer an articulate and evocative homiletical witness.

However, one historic voice has been strangely quiet in the current homiletical revival in the pulpits of the long-established denominations. To our knowledge, few in these churches are giving significant attention to the sermon that moves through the text verse by verse, essentially providing a running commentary on the text.[14] This type of preaching goes by different names in different eras and in different books and articles about preaching. It is sometimes called expository preaching, or textual preaching, or continuous exposition, or verse by verse preaching.[15] By sermon as running commentary, we mean preaching that centers in exposition of the ancient and contemporary significance of a biblical text by following the structure of the text itself. The sermon unfolds much like a commentary on the Bible; the preacher interprets the passage sense unit by sense unit, sometimes word by word.[16] Sometimes the preacher draws out the significance of the text for today as the sermon unfolds; sometimes the preacher identifies contemporary implications at the end of the sermon.

Preaching verse by verse has shown remarkable power to help congregations in many different times and places to encounter the living God. Its roots are as old as the Jewish people of antiquity. However, it can be as contemporary as the hair still damp from the shower on the heads of some of those in today's sanctuary.

We do not advocate preaching verse by verse as the only needle on the preacher's homiletical compass. The current homiletical revival correctly emphasizes that specific occasions call for homilies that are shaped, in both content and form, for specific occasions. The sermon as running commentary takes its place as one generative homiletical venue alongside others. A critical task of the preacher is to assay the situation of the congregation in order to determine the style and content for a sermon that seems fitting.

However, we hasten to a qualification. The newer approaches to preaching are exciting and imaginative, but they do not yet have a proven record of being able to encourage the biblical literacy and theological depth necessary to sustain Christian identity, community, and mission. Indeed, our observation is that the newer approaches are easily susceptible to misuse. Preachers can become so intent on their own cleverness that style supersedes substance. As we point out in the first two chapters, the sermon as running commentary has repeatedly shown the ability to help a preacher and congregation grow in Christian maturity (providing, of course, that the preaching is well done).

In chapter 1, we note the attractiveness and timeliness of preaching in the mode of running commentary. We observe that preachers from many different theological perspectives can preach in this medium and honor the full range of their theological commitments. Chapter 2 offers representative voices from the long and powerful tradition of preaching as continuous exposition. Chapter 3 enumerates practical considerations for preparing a sermon in this style. We offer five sample exegeses, drawn from different genres of biblical literature, to illustrate the wide-ranging applicability of verse by verse preaching. Chapter 4 develops options for structuring the sermon in this genre, and lays out five sample sermons from our own preaching that illustrate treatments of different kinds of biblical texts. The sermons are briefly annotated so that readers can know what we are attempting to do in these sermons. Chapter 5 offers tips for helping this type of preaching be fresh, vital, and engaging. Chapter 6 considers occasions when running commentary may be an especially suggestive mode of preaching.

Each author wrote first drafts of selected chapters. We both then worked together to revise and refine each chapter. Gilbert Bartholomew did the primary work on chapters 3 and 5. Ronald Allen did the initial drafts of chapters 1, 2, and 6. Each prepared two sermons for chapter 4. Linda Milavec also contributed a sermon to chapter 4.

At its best, preaching verse by verse can help preachers join the writer of 1 John in witnessing to what they have heard, what they have seen, and what they have touched with their own hands concerning the word of life (1 John 1:1). In so doing, the congregation's communion with God may deepen and strengthen.

1

The Attractiveness
of Preaching Verse by Verse

As noted in the introduction, we have great confidence in the power of preaching in the mode of running commentary. However, some of our clergy colleagues are skeptical when they hear about this proposal. A friend, a pastor in one of the long-established denominations and schooled in the historical-critical and literary-critical methods of biblical interpretation, sums up her uneasiness with this way of preaching. "Why should I be interested in preaching that is dull, dull, dull? The only people I know who use running commentary are television preachers who say some things I do not believe. I won't prance in front of a congregation brandishing a limp-back Bible. And those preachers assume that the congregation is made up of passive sponges, just waiting to soak up the water that the preacher splashes at them. This style asks nothing of me as a creative communicator or the congregation as active listeners. I could just read from *The New Interpreter's Bible.*"

We now explore why, and show how, preaching as running commentary can be an exciting option for this pastor and for today's congregation. In addition to providing a positive rationale for this approach, we hope to allay the skepticism represented by our friend. A preacher can partake of the blessings of running commentary without sacrifice of theological or ethical substance and without compromise of integrity. After developing the major strengths of this approach, we turn to an evaluation of its weaknesses.

CONGREGATIONS
RESPOND POSITIVELY

James Fish is an administrator at a theological seminary. For the past ten years, he has served several interim pastorates. During these assignments, he has experimented with how the congregations respond to different types of preaching. Working through a text one verse at a time was one experiment: "These 'expository Bible studies' have consistently drawn the strongest positive response from the congregations."[1] Fish concludes that many congregations feel a need to learn the Bible. Indeed, some had "given up trying to remember my well-intentioned but too crafty sermons. Perhaps they had also given up on adult Bible classes or found the anonymity of worship more comfortable than a class setting. The reasons are, no doubt, many."[2]

Fish's anecdotal experience is reinforced by the wider research of Lyle Schaller. Schaller has investigated many growing congregations that have a high percentage of relatively young members with a high degree of commitment to the mission of the church and who believe that they are maturing in faith. He finds that in such congregations, the sermon usually has a teaching character.[3] Frequently the preaching takes the form of verse by verse exposition of a biblical text.

Many people in North America associate encounter with the Bible with encounter with the transcendent. When the preacher deals seriously with the Bible, many in the congregation have the impression that the preacher is dealing significantly with God and life.

Systematic programs for the study of the Bible (such as Kerygma, Bethel, ABIL, the materials from the Mission for Biblical Literacy) often attract large numbers of people. This suggests that many Christians today feel a need to study the Bible and to deepen their awareness of God. Running commentary can help respond to this felt need.

Some leaders in the field of preaching suggest that pastors need to preach short sermons and that we need to divide each sermon into sound-bite-size chunks so that the sermon will be brief enough and fast paced enough to keep the attention of the MTV generation. However, when a preacher is an energetic communicator who deals with matters of significance, the congregation can become invested in a surprisingly long sermon. This is particularly true of running commentary. Lyle Schaller finds that "an expository sermon may hold people's attention for 25 to 45 minutes."[4] We are not calling for long sermons, especially when the congregation is not socialized to expect one. (A dull, insignificant sermon is too long, no matter what its genre and length.) But we highlight the possibility that lively running commentary can attract and hold people's attention.

RUNNING COMMENTARY AND MOMENTS OF CHRISTIAN RENEWAL

Sermons in the form of running commentary have often contributed to regeneration of Christian faith and life. Augustine favored this mode of preaching in his reemphasis on the priority of grace as the center of Christian existence. At the time of the Reformation, both Luther and Calvin preached in running commentary almost daily. On the United States frontier of the early 1800s, the Restoration movement led by Thomas and Alexander Campbell gave priority to this pattern of Sunday study, "examining the different books [of the Bible] in regular succession."[5] At the beginning of the twentieth century, Karl Barth excited a vital theological conversation through his commentary on Romans.

In our own time, many congregations on the evangelical end of the theological spectrum gather around such preaching. Many of these congregations are growing in size. The congregations tend to be young in age, to enjoy a high percentage of members who attend worship, to have an intense commitment to mission, and to feel that they are deepening in faith.[6] The sermon alone does not generate these vital qualities; they result from the congregational life system. But such running commentary helps the congregation feel that they encounter transcendent reality.

The turn to running commentary will not result automatically in the revitalization of Christian faith and witness. But its participation in previous discoveries and rediscoveries of Christian

identity suggest the possibility that it could help strengthen today's congregation.

OVERCOMING BIBLICAL
AND THEOLOGICAL ILLITERACY

As is well known, many Christians in the long-established denominations today have difficulty navigating the Bible and Christian doctrine. Running commentary can help the congregation
become acquainted with the Bible by drawing the congregation
into the world of the Bible through attention to the detail of particular biblical texts. The congregation can become immersed in
the language, imagery, associations, and movement of the text.

Through running commentary the congregation can have the
maximum opportunity to discern and evaluate the text's specific
claims. Working through a text verse by verse and word by word
can be especially useful when the text is hard to understand. Romans 9–11, for instance, is especially dense. Working through
those chapters segment by segment allows the congregation (and
the preacher!) to appreciate the depth of Paul's struggle and the
significance of his conclusion.

When the pastor locates a particular passage in its historical, literary, and theological contexts (as we advocate in chapter 3), this
style of preaching encourages the congregation to become familiar
with the larger chronology of the Bible, as well as its literary and
theological worlds. In the process, the listening community can get
a sense of how the individual passage fits into the larger biblical
and Christian worlds.

In addition to encouraging familiarity with the content of the
Bible, sermons in running commentary model a significant way to
approach, understand, and evaluate biblical material. Running
commentary can help the listeners recognize (and develop) responsible methods of biblical interpretation, theological analysis,
and hermeneutical connection. When preached in the context of
an adequate theological method, sermons in this mode can help
the church learn better how to think theologically.

The form of running commentary can help preachers honor the

integrity of the text. Some preachers begin sermon preparation with a particular passage in mind, but then quickly extrapolate a theme or topic that becomes the real focus of the sermon. The text becomes a springboard to the topic. Running commentary can help the preacher deal with the specific content of a text and the issues raised by the text.

DRAWING ON CONTEMPORARY BIBLICAL INTERPRETATION

When preaching in the genre of continuous exposition, the preacher can draw upon key insights from the full range of the contemporary, critical interpretation of the Bible.[7] A simultaneous challenge for the preacher is to judge how much data from critical analysis to bring into the sermon and how to make it interesting enough to hold the listener's attention.

Historical criticism has been widely (and often properly) criticized in the last decades. Nonetheless, aspects of historical study still have value for the preacher. The sermon can include historical criticism's recovery of possible meanings of cultural assumptions, words, and practices in the eras of the Bible. Recent sociological exegesis can help us understand the social worlds of the Bible. Tradition history frequently can help us understand how (and why) a text came into its present form. It can help the preacher identify how a text could have been heard in the ancient world. In some cases, the historical critic can help reconstruct the historical situation within which texts came to expression. This can be illuminating when the context can be identified with some certainty (e.g., the exilic setting of Isaiah 40–55).

The newer modes of literary criticism can help the preacher and congregation enter the literary world within the text (i.e., the text's view of reality).[8] Some literary critics, such as those who practice the New Literary Criticism, eschew reconstructing the history of the text and focus altogether on the text itself; the text is interpreted on its own terms. But most literary criticism believes that it can be enriched by insights from historical recovery. Rhetorical criticism and reader-response criticism can lead the preacher to

grasp the effect that the text was intended to have among its ancient receivers. The ancient purpose of a passage (as revealed
through various modes of literary criticism) may suggest possible
purposes for the sermon. Isaiah 40, for instance, was intended to
rekindle the community's confidence in God; that purpose may
serve the contemporary congregation. As a part of the running
commentary, the preacher could explain this purpose and why it is
a credible one for today's church.

The preacher can make use of the hermeneutic of suspicion and
of ideology criticism in running commentary.[9] These disciplines
seek to bring to light the vested interests that are often a part of
the creation of our sacred texts. These perspectives attempt to
uncover ways in which texts have been shaped (and used) so as to
preserve authority and privilege in the hands of some in the community, often at the expense of the marginalization, oppression,
and abuse of others. For instance, feminist theologians often call
attention to patriarchal bias in the scriptures. By looking closely at
the nuances of a text, a preacher can often help the congregation
see these qualities in sharp relief. The pastor can also use suspicion
and ideology criticism to unmask ways in which the Christian tradition (and the congregation) have used the text (or other related
dimensions of Christian doctrine or practice) to protect its privilege or to enforce patterns of oppression, marginalization, or abuse.

Running commentary can be compatible with the recent emphasis on orality and aurality in biblical interpretation. Scholars in this
movement call attention to the distinctive perspectives that emerge
when one hears and interprets a text as an oral-aural expression (the
original medium for many biblical texts) and the differences that
emerge when the text is translated from the oral-aural realm into
print.[10] When preaching a running commentary, the preacher can
easily explain these insights. Other interpreters go a step further by
encouraging the lector to present the scripture lesson in the service
of worship as an oral-aural event. Instead of reading from the printed
text, the lector speaks the text, usually without notes, with vibrant
inflection, so that the text comes alive in face to face and ear to ear
encounter.[11] When apropos, the text can be spoken in this fashion
in preparation for the sermon as running commentary. In chapter 5,

we will suggest that members of the congregation should be asked to bring their Bibles to worship so that they can pay close attention to the biblical text itself during the preaching. However, the congregation may not always need the printed text; some biblical passages or sermons may call for the sermon itself to continue the oral-aural style of the presentation of the text. In this case, the congregation would leave their Bibles closed as they participate in the sermon.[12] In these matters, today's preachers are twice blessed, for we can take advantage of the media (oral-aural or print) that seem most promising for a particular sermon.

SERVING A WIDE RANGE OF THEOLOGIES

In today's church, the sermon as running commentary is associated primarily with preachers who have an evangelical or fundamentalist theological orientation. This association is natural. Evangelicals regard the Bible as the inspired word of God that imparts utterly essential revelation to the church and the world. The church must understand the biblical text in its fullness in order to grasp the completeness of divine revelation. Indeed, in a sense for the evangelical, theology is explaining the Bible and drawing out its implications. Running commentary is only one of many homiletical modes in evangelical circles, but it is an instinctive vehicle for evangelical theology.

Running commentary can be powered by other theological positions as well.[13] All Christian theologies respect the Bible, draw from it, and wish to hear it in its fullness and integrity. The text is a genuine Other. In order to respect the integrity of the Other, theologian, preacher, and congregation need to be as attuned as possible to the nuances of the text. Running commentary provides maximum opportunity for acquaintance.

The liberation theologian works through the text with one eye looking for the news of God's liberating power. Do the bits and pieces of the passage come together to enhance our understanding of God's liberating will? With the other eye, the liberation theologian uses the hermeneutic of suspicion to ask whether the text has been used oppressively in the history of the church or whether the text itself may contain oppressive elements (or both). Verse by verse Bible study has been particularly important in Latin America in the base communities.

Running commentary could be a close friend of postliberal theology.[14] This theological orientation (associated with theologians such as Hans Frei, George Lindbeck, Stanley Hauerwas, William Placher, and William Willimon) assumes that the preacher's task is to *describe* the world from the Christian point of view, especially as that point of view is manifest in the Bible and in Christian doctrine and tradition. Postliberal theologians believe, in contrast to the reversionary theologians (who are discussed below), "The theologian's job is not to make the gospel credible to the modern world, but *to make the world credible to the gospel.*"[15] The preacher describes the world as it is narrated in the Bible and as the contemporary world can be shaped by the biblical one. Running commentary could help the postliberal congregation become attuned to the subtleties of the biblical world as described through a biblical text.

Reversionary theology, associated with such theologians as David Tracy, Sallie McFague, Marjorie Suchocki, John Cobb, and Gordon Kaufmann, seeks to explore how Christian faith can be an intellectually credible (and morally compelling) possibility for contemporary people. The pastor discerns points at which the Bible and Christian tradition are instructive for the contemporary world by correlating basic realities of the Bible and Christian doctrine and practice with similar realities today. The pastor also criticizes Christian tradition and practice on the basis of contemporary insights, sometimes calling for reformulation of Christian perspectives on faith and life. Indeed, the text can lead the congregation to be critical of its view of reality and to reformulate its understanding of contemporaneity. Running commentary can become an event of mutual critical correlation as the preacher elucidates the components of the biblical text in the light of the text's possibilities for correlation and for criticism.

USING CONTEMPORARY EMPHASES IN HOMILETICS

In the last twenty years, homiletics has emphasized the importance of inductive movement, narrative, and the use of imagery in preaching.[16] When preaching in running commentary, the sermon can often manifest these qualities. This can be true especially when the biblical text is itself a narrative or image or has an inductive character. The exposition follows the text so that the sermon follows the movement of the text. The preacher interprets the details of the text so that the congregation can appreciate (and enter into) the text. In the case of a narrative, the sermon can unfold with the plot of the story and can reach a climax (if fitting) at the same juncture as the narrative. In the case of an image, the interpretation of the text can help the listeners enter into the world of the image. An inductive text that reserves its point, conclusion, or application for the end of the passage (or that implies its point, conclusion, or application) suggests that the preacher follow the text in a similar way.

The preacher can also make use of narrative and image as a component of the exposition. At judicious junctures of the sermon, the preacher can tell a story or create an image. At one level, such developments may simply illustrate the exegesis or hermeneutical interpretation of the text. By hearing the story or the image, the congregation can get a clear picture of the preacher's exegetical or hermeneutical point. At a deeper level, such moments may create worlds within the sermon. Entering into the world of the story or the image can touch the congregation at all its levels of understanding: in mind and heart, in the depths of the congregational gestalt. Indeed, the congregation can experience the world from the standpoint of the story or image. In the pulpit of a sensitive, artistic preacher, running commentary can become an aesthetic event.

Of course, the preacher cannot assume that every text is a fully adequate expression of the gospel. As we note below, a few texts have theological, moral, or intellectual problems. In such cases, it is not enough for the congregation to identify with the passage; the pastor is called to help the community make a critical evaluation of the witness of the passage. However, beyond critical evaluation, full Christian preaching articulates the good news of the gospel. Narrative and image can often help the sermon move negative to positive. One set of narratives and images could be a part of the discovery of the problematic elements of the passage and another set could create a gospel-shaped world into which the congregation can enter as an alternative to the world of the text.

PREACHING AGAINST A TEXT

A few biblical texts are so theologically or morally problematic that the preacher is called to preach against them.[17] These texts often deny God's love to some in the text; some such texts even advocate brutality in God's name. The classic example is Psalm 137:9: "Happy shall they be who take your little ones [i.e., the babies of the Babylonians] and dash them against the rock!" In order to be faithful to the gospel of God's universal love for all and God's will for justice for all, the preacher must say that such passages do not measure up to the fullness of our understanding of God and God's will for the world. Many congregations are unaccustomed to sermons against the text. Running commentary allows the congregation to explore in detail the reasons for preaching a sermon that seeks to correct the witness of a text.

Preachers and congregations who are uneasy with this possibility might be comforted by remembering that its antecedents can be found within scripture itself. To offer an oversimplified example, the Deuteronomic theologians think that obedience results in blessing, while disobedience calls forth a curse. The book of Job objects that blessing and curse cannot so easily be correlated with obedience and disobedience. To take another example, the Synoptic Gospels generally assume that the resurrection of the dead will take place as a singular event, in the future, as a part of the apocalypse. The Fourth Gospel criticizes this point of view, and claims that the resurrection is already being realized in the present. "I am the resurrection and the life." (See John 11:17–27, especially vv. 24–25.) Many of the rabbis argued with sacred texts, and with each other regarding how to interpret sacred passages. From these examples, we learn that it is important for preacher and congregation to bring our questions and misgivings into the process of preparing the sermon. By facing these matters directly, we are forced to think clearly about what we do and do not believe.

A BASIC MOVEMENT
FOR THE SERMON AND A PLACE TO START

The preacher must determine not only what to say but how to say it. When preaching in the genre of continuous exposition, the movement of the biblical text provides the preacher with a basic pattern of movement for the sermon. Of course, the preacher must make sure that the sermon starts in a way that can engage the listeners, moves in a way that the congregation can track easily, includes experiences that enhance the purpose of the sermon, and ends in a way that is congruent with the aim of the message. But the pastor can give minimal attention to matters of structure and form and can concentrate on matters of exegetical and theological content. The preacher has one less decision to make.

When preaching a series of sermons from a single book (e.g., 2 Corinthians) or corpus (e.g., the Deuteronomic theologians), the preacher also has a place to start. The pastor does not have to explore different possibilities for a sermon. The preacher can take the time that would have gone into selecting a text or topic and invest it directly in the preparation of the sermon. Of course, even when preaching such a series, the preacher needs to weigh each week whether the preselected text and purpose for the sermon fit the congregation and the context.

CAUTIONS

Running commentary does have its dangers. These dangers are not inherent weaknesses, but the weaknesses can easily occur. The preacher cannot assume that running commentary will fit every occasion in a congregation's life. As we note in chapter 6, it fits some occasions and needs better than others. Further, the sermon can become boring, especially if it drifts into a monotonous procession of archaeological information. When concentrating on the details of the text, the preacher can lose sight of the main message of the passage.

By drilling deeply into the single unit of scripture (or by dwelling for long periods of time in a single book, author, or corpus), running commentary can allow preachers to dwell on their favorite parts of the Bible to the exclusion of other parts. The same thing can be true of the elements of Christian doctrine suggested by the passages of scripture on which they dwell. Preacher and congregation thereby can be denied the benefits of other parts of the Bible (and the benefits of the therapeutic struggle with the difficult voices of scripture) and Christian doctrine.

A preacher sometimes may become so mesmerized by working with a passage in depth that the preacher allows the text to chart the course of the sermon without taking account of the larger theological map within which the sermon needs to make its journey. A pastor can forget to bring the text into a larger theological conversation concerning the theological witness of the text, its faithfulness to the gospel, and its adequacy for the contemporary world. Even worse, ministers can easily retroject their own theologies into the text. The integrity of the text (and its possibility to speak to preacher and community as a genuine Other) can be compromised.

If the sermon is not lively, it easily can become too long. Even a lively sermon may be too long if it exceeds the length of time the congregation has been socialized to associate with the sermon. The preacher needs to discern those aspects of exegetical, theological, and hermeneutical discovery that are essential to a particular sermon and highlight those, while downplaying or omitting other information. Such pruning can be painful, but it is often essential if the sermon is to have the maximum opportunity to engage the community.

At its best, preaching verse by verse focuses our energy for depth exploration and engagement with the world of the Bible. It provides a means whereby the congregation can consider how the biblical word can help us interpret and shape our worlds from the perspective of the gospel.

The Lively Tradition of Preaching Verse by Verse

Family stories often help us know who we are. When I was a child, my father told me how my grandfather and he had worked together to clear a plot of land in the Ozark Mountains for a homestead. They worked from dawn to dark. They used dynamite to blast rocks and tree stumps. My father transferred that driving pattern of work to high school, college, and professional school. When I heard these family stories, they generated a similar energy in me.

This chapter is such a family story. It recalls pastors in earlier generations who have preached in the mode of running commentary. Such familiarity does not provide a format and content that a minister can mechanically imitate. But a living memory can help us think about how we can adapt this approach to our own time, place, and theological viewpoints. It can help us remember that systematic exposition has had significant capacity to bring communities in notably different situations to fresh awareness of the presence, purpose, and power of the living God. Remembering earlier commentary preachers helps give us a sense of family connection; we become aware that we are part of a significant (and positive) history and community. Awareness of the diversity that has characterized this practice can help ministers today recognize that we have considerable creative freedom. And it can strengthen our confidence that this style of preaching can be an effective witness to the gospel.

In this chapter, we recall representative clergy who have preached in the mode of running commentary and provide brief selections from sermons.

FORESHADOWING IN THE FIRST TESTAMENT

The First Testament (often called the Old Testament or the Hebrew Bible) does not contain extensive examples of running commentary (that is, detailed passages in which First Testament writers comment, in segment by segment fashion, on earlier texts). However, the running commentary is a natural outgrowth of inclinations in the Hebrew Bible. The First Testament was formed by a process of interpretation and reinterpretation.[1] Traditions, originally oral and disparate, were refined and brought into proximity. Gradually they became formalized, written, and the subject of exposition. A later community often would be faced with a text that was important to the community's identity and behavior, but whose implications were not immediately clear. The meaning of the text or tradition was clarified and its significance drawn out.[2]

An obvious example: Stories of Samuel, Saul, David, and Solomon were noteworthy narratives in the religious life of pre-exilic Israel.[3] The Deuteronomic theologians gathered these tales into the books we call 1 and 2 Samuel and 1 and 2 Kings. These books interpret these stories from a Deuteronomic point of view. In turn, 1 and 2 Chronicles give a homiletical reinterpretation of much of the story told in the books of Samuel and Kings.[4] They give an exposition of these books through the lens of priestly theology by means of retelling (and reframing) the older stories.

Michael Fishbane stresses that the communities of the First Testament are exegetical at heart, as they seek to explain the significance of ancient traditions for each new generation.[5] Such "exegetical orientation," he contends, is basic to the "internal transformation of the historical religions. Significantly, the Teacher of Righteousness at Qumran, and Jesus, and Paul, and all the religious reformers that come to mind, presented themselves as the authentic *interpreters* of the religions which they represented."[6] The interpreters typically move within the stream of the exegetical conventions, hermeneutical assumptions, and theological points of view typical of their times.

QUMRAN AND MIDRASH AND THE FIRST FULLY DEVELOPED RUNNING COMMENTARY

Running commentary first emerged as a distinct mode at Qumran (circa 130 B.C.E. to 70 C.E.).[7] The Qumran commentators cite the first words of a text and then comment on their significance. The exposition continues in this systematic fashion. The community at Qumran believed that it was living in the last days before the apocalyptic cataclysm that would destroy the present evil world and would result in a revitalized cosmos. The commentators found this scenario prefigured in biblical texts.[8] The exposition seeks to help the community discern its identity, situation, and mission in the light of the text as read through Qumranian theology.

The following excerpt from the commentary on Habakkuk illustrates this exegetical program. The Wicked Priest is an archenemy of the community (likely Jonathan, a high priest despised by the Qumranites). "The poor" is a self-designation for the community. Material in square brackets is physically missing from the fragment and has been supplied by the translator.

> [*For the violence done to Lebanon shall overwhelm you, and the destruction of the beasts*] *shall terrify you, because of the blood of men and the violence done to the land, the city, and all its inhabitants* (*Habakkuk 2:17*).
>
> Interpreted, this saying concerns the Wicked Priest, inasmuch as he shall be paid the reward which he himself tendered to the poor. For *Lebanon* is the Council of the Community; and the *beasts* are the simple of Judah who keep the Law. As he himself plotted the destruction of the poor, so will God condemn him to destruction. And as for that which he said, *Because of the blood of the city and the violence done to the land:* interpreted, *the city* is Jerusalem where the Wicked Priest committed abominable deeds and defiled the Temple of God.

> *The violence done to the land:* these are the cities of Ju-
> dah where he robbed the Poor of their possessions.[9]

The expositor does not aim to interpret the prophecy in its historical or literary settings. The commentator seeks to encourage
the community with a theological-allegorical reading of the text.
Nonetheless, the principle is clearly illustrated that to understand
the fullness of revelation, the community must understand the fullness of the text.

A similar genre, though animated by a different theology, comes
to the surface in midrash. Scholars have sometimes imprecisely
used the term *midrash* for almost any act of rendering a sacred text
meaningful to a later community. In recent years, however, a growing number of scholars agree that Gary Porton offers a useful de-
limitation. Midrash is "a type of literature, oral or written, which
stands in direct relationship to a fixed, canonical text, considered
to be the authoritative and the revealed word of God by the
midrashist and his audience, and in which this canonical text is ex-
plicitly cited or clearly alluded to."[10] Midrash reaches its peak of
development in the activity and literature of the rabbis.

Under Porton's umbrella, scholars identify a vast number of different genres of midrash. These include Targumim (interpretive
translations of the Hebrew Bible), retellings of the Hebrew Bible,
general consideration of texts (such as Philo's philosophical-
theological commentary on Genesis), or detailed interpretations of
legal and narrative texts.[11] The midrashic literature with which
Christians are most likely to be acquainted are the Mishnah and
the Talmud.

Running commentary is a genre of midrash. In sequential fashion, the rabbis interpret biblical texts according to their own exegetical and hermeneutical assumptions. Other rabbis add to the
commentary (occasionally disputing one another). Hence, rabbinic
midrash often becomes a conversation about the proper interpretation of the text. The contemporary community takes its place in
the conversation. At its height rabbinic commentary can be understood to re-present revelation.[12]

Such expository and conversational characteristics are clear in the following brief excerpt from a commentary on the biblical book of Numbers. The biblical passage instructs the priests and Levites concerning proper behavior in the sanctuary. The rabbis debate whether this instruction relates to the practice of the Levites' singing.

> *But, they shall not draw near to the holy vessels* (Num. 18:3). This [refers to] the ark and the portion containing the ark, [for it is said,] *But they shall not go in to look upon the dismantling of the holy things even for a moment [lest they die]* (Num. 4:20). Rabbi Nathan says: "Here [we find] a hint in the Torah concerning the Levites' singing; but it was specifically mentioned [only] by Ezra." Rabbi Hananyah the son of Rabbi Joseph's brother says: "There is no need [for Rabbi Nathan's interpretation], for behold, already it was said, *Moses spoke and God answered him in a voice* (Ex. 19:19). Here we have a hint in the Torah concerning the [Levites'] singing."[13]

From the standpoint of today's historical or literary criticism, the discovery of references to Levitical singing in the texts cited from Numbers or Exodus seems eisegetical. But catchword associations were common in rabbinic hermeneutics. Such practices may not provide an exact model for today's preacher. But the pastor who takes the occasion of running commentary to dispute the possible interpretations of a biblical text stands in a long and honorable company.

ORIGEN AND THE THREEFOLD NEEDS OF HEARERS

Writers in the Second Testament consistently interpret the First Testament in order to explain the Christian gospel.[14] Romans 4, for instance, is essentially an exegesis of selections from Genesis 12–17. Much of the early Christian literature beyond the Bible draws upon the Old Testament (and other Jewish and non-Jewish sources) as a part of the grounding of their witness. However, in the first two centuries of the common era, we find few examples of continuous exposition of lengthy pieces of sacred tradition from Christian hands.[15]

Origen (185–254) is the first Christian preacher to make extensive use of the genre of running commentary. Origen's biblical interpretation and preaching shows the influence of the popular Alexandrian philosophy in which he was schooled. Origen often discusses texts from three perspectives: the literal, the mystical, and the allegorical (sometimes referred to as the body, soul, and spirit of the Bible, or as the literal, moral, and mystical senses). These descriptions refer less to "separate and self-contained senses of the same text" than to "an order of doctrines which corresponds to the progressive steps of the Christian's movement toward perfection."[16] The preacher draws out the level of interpretation that meets the needs of the hearers.

The literal reading is interested less in the facticity in the text than in offering simple and unlettered hearers an interpretation of the text that they can understand and apply. The intermediate level of interpretation is for the person who is advancing toward perfection but whose insight is still limited. The fully allegorical reading is for the mature.[17] While Origen's allegorical extrapolations sometimes seem utterly arbitrary (and even bizarre) to today's historical or literary critic, we need to remember that they are consonant with Origen's world of thought.

A typical homily from Origen contains four elements. Origen divides the text into units for interpretation (usually each unit comprises about a verse). Then he treats each unit in four steps: (1) he refers to the biblical words to be interpreted, (2) he states the theological context within which to understand the materials, (3) he elucidates individual words and thoughts, and (4) he incorporates the hearer into the text so that the text can be specifically applied to the situation of the hearer.[18] Sermons on Old Testament texts usually repeat this pattern as the sermon moves verse by verse through a chapter. Sermons on New Testament texts sometimes omit step 4 from the exposition of the single units and present it as the conclusion to the sermon.[19]

Origen's exegetical and homiletical programs are powered by a single driving concern: for the interpreter to reveal the Logos who is present throughout scripture. As Karen Torjesen comments, "That the teachings of Scripture are the teachings of Christ comes to its most powerful expression in the fact that Christ is actually made present through his teachings so that hearing the teachings of Christ is to be in the presence of Christ himself."[20] Hence, Origen nearly always helps the hearers locate themselves in the text.[21] They are transposed into the world of the Bible so that the word (Christ) can act upon them.[22]

We can see Origen's homiletical, exegetical, and theological program come to compact expression in the following segment from a homily on Numbers 33:8. Origen takes the journey of the Israelites from Egypt through the wilderness to speak of a double exodus: (1) when believers leave their Gentile lives for life in the law of God; (2) when, allegorically described, the soul ascends from the body and Egypt (this world with its ignorance) toward perfection (the promised land).

Next, they set out from Iroth and pass through the midst of the Red Sea, and camp at the Bitter Waters (Num. 33:8; Marah). We have said that the time of starting places is a time of dangers. How hard a temptation it is to pass through the midst of the sea, to see the waves rise piled up, to hear the noise and rumbling of the raging waters! But if you follow Moses, that is, the Law of God, the waters will become for you walls on the right and left, and you will find a path on dry ground in the midst of the sea (cf. Ex. 14:22). Moreover, it can happen that the heavenly journey that we say the soul takes may hold peril of waters; waves may be found there. For one part of the waters is above the heavens and another part under heaven (cf. Gen. 1:7). For the time being, we endure the waves and the billows of the waters under heaven. And God will see whether they can be quiet and calm and not stirred up by any winds blowing upon them. But meanwhile, when we come to the crossing of the sea, although we see Pharaoh and the Egyptians in pursuit, we shall in no way be alarmed, shall have no fear of them, no terror. Let us simply believe in the only true God and His Son Jesus Christ whom He sent (cf. Jn. 17:3). And if it is said that

the people believed in God and in His servant Moses, we also
believe in this way in Moses, that is, the Law of God and the
prophets. Therefore, stand fast and in a little while you will
see the Egyptians lying on the seashore (Ex. 14:30). And
when you see them lying there, rise up and sing songs to the
Lord, and praise Him who sank the horse and his rider in the
Red Sea (cf. Ex. 15:1ff).[23]

The listeners join the Israelites in crossing the Red Sea. But if
they believe in Christ, they need not fear.

Running commentary also appears (though with less attention
to allegory) in some of the sermons of the highly influential
preaching of John Chrysostom (circa 347–407)[24] and Augustine
(354–430).[25]

RUNNING COMMENTARY IN LUTHER AND CALVIN

In the centuries prior to Luther (1483–1546) and Calvin
(1509–1564), preaching became increasingly sophisticated deco-
rative rhetoric, combined with highly philosophical content and a
minimum of attention to scripture. Luther put his lever and ful-
crum against the trend and called for a reemphasis on preaching
from the Bible. "Listeners are to hear God speaking in his saving
power and presence in sermons. The aim of the sermon is therefore to help hearers understand the *text*, not just a religious truth.
Its goal is that God may speak a gracious word through a text so
that people may be given faith or be strengthened in faith by the
Holy Spirit."[26]

Luther takes a selection from the Bible, locates the heart of that
selection, and brings that thought to life for the congregation.
Typically, Luther's sermons had little introduction; Luther states
directly the center of the text (and, consequently, the center of the
sermon). He frequently follows the movement and language of the
text itself, not imposing a structure on the text but allowing the sermon to unfold in pattern of thought in the text itself.[27] Luther usually moves verse by verse through the text, with the exposition of
the individual verses controlled by the main point that he has announced at the beginning of the sermon.[28] Thus, Luther's preach-

ing is marked by simplicity, with minimal attention to artistry and cleverness and with maximum focus on bringing justification by grace to bear on the situation of the listeners through the text.

Luther's style is evident, below, in this part of a sermon on 2 Corinthians 3:4–6. At the beginning of the sermon, he recounts the setting in the time of Paul: Interloper preachers have entered the Corinthian community and have challenged Paul's authority. Paul needs to reestablish his authority in the community.

So Paul here hardly knows what to do. "Do we need, as some do, letters of recommendation to you or from you? You yourselves are our letters of recommendation" (2 Cor. 3:1–2). His words are kindly for the sake of the devout, who have the gospel in their hearts and have not been defected, not for those who are evangelical in name but are devils nevertheless. But he says, "Such is the confidence that we have through Christ toward God" (2 Cor. 3:4). And that we can set down and let stand. If I can't convert the whole crowd, then I'll gain one or two. This is our confidence: when we have preached, it will not have been in vain. If the townsmen, peasants, and the big fellows don't want it, let them leave it; let them go; they will see for themselves that they will regret it. And then there are some who always know better, like the sectarians and our young noblemen, who can handle it better than we can. But when it comes to a showdown, they turn out to be scamps and traitors. The townsmen, the fellows who, when they have read one book are full of the Holy Spirit, are the worst. If I were to follow my own impulse I would say, "Let the damned devil be your preacher!" So I have often thought, but I cannot bring myself to do it. But then confidence returns and we say, let happen what may, we still have our confidence through Christ.[29]

The preacher's confidence is in the Word of God. The Word is preeminently the news of justification by grace through faith.

For Calvin, the minister is called to help the congregation become educated in the Christian life. The church is a school. The preacher is a teacher. The Holy Spirit uses the sermon to build up the congregation.[30] "When Calvin is talking about preaching the word that meets us at every turn is 'teaching'; indeed, this is very often used as a synonym for 'preaching.'"[31] The sermon is to expound the Bible, whose heart is "the gracious self-revelation of the hidden God" and humankind's "grateful acceptance and submission to it."[32] The preached Word can be both a sign of God's presence and a means through which Christ rules in the community. Indeed, when empowered by the Holy Spirit, the sermon has the power "to accomplish its commands and purposes." This power can effect judgment as well as salvation.[33] Like Luther, Calvin devalued homiletical artistry and cleverness, insisting instead on straightforward interpretation.

The exposition of the Bible is the heart of such preaching. In his preaching, Calvin worked his way systematically through whole books of the Bible. Calvin sometimes preached multiple sermons (on successive days) on a single verse or passage. Calvin began a series of sermons on a biblical book with a sermon that discussed the main themes of the book. Calvin would then move passage by passage through the book.[34]

When expounding a particular passage, the sermon divides into similar units of interpretation. In each section, Calvin states the part of the text that is the immediate focus, usually a verse or part of a verse. He then explains the meaning of that part of the text. As necessary, he engages in word study, in grammatical analysis, in historical recollection, in connecting the segment of scripture to other parts of the Bible, to Christian history, or to Christian doctrine. The discussion ends with an application that fits the situation of the listeners.[35] Calvin's approach is not stiff and wooden: "The sermons are like rivers, moving strongly in one direction, alive with eddies and cross-currents, now thundering in cataracts, now a calm mirror of the banks and the sky; but never still, never stagnant."[36] Throughout, Calvin speaks in "familiar style," that is, as person to person, "so that we may know that it is *God* who is speaking to *us*."[37]

These emphases can be recognized in a sermon on Luke 2:9–14 (the visit of the shepherds to the infant Jesus). Calvin's positive evaluation of the Jewish community also comes to expression here.

For the rest, the Angel does not content himself with saying that he announces a joy, but says that it is *a great joy,* yea, *which shall be to all people.* Consider this carefully. For if this word had not been added, we should imagine that what St. Luke narrates applied only to the shepherds. But this joy was to be shed upon all people. It is true that the Angel is speaking of the Jews, for they were the elect people. But now the partition is broken down, says St. Paul, and Jesus Christ by the preaching of the Gospel proclaims peace to those who were formerly afar off and to those who were nigh. The Jews were allied to God when He adopted them in the person of Abraham—which adoption He confirmed by His Law. But now, although we were afar off, yet God came to us and wished this Gospel of reconciliation to be general. This is why it is said that Jesus Christ proclaims in the Gospel peace to those who formerly were far from God and had no knowledge of Him. Well, then, since it is here declared to us by the Angel that we ought to rejoice in the coming of our Lord Jesus Christ (not in the ordinary sense of the word but meaning that we should be transported with joy,) we must make this doctrine profitable to us.[38]

Calvin then uses the shepherds to apply the text to the listeners. Their "worldly condition" was not improved as a result of their receiving the news of God's grace. They continued to be "cold at night and hot in the day, and were ill-clothed. Nevertheless, they rejoiced. . . . And here see how we must be conformed to their example. That is, although the Gospel does not increase our wealth and honours, although it brings us neither enjoyments nor pleasures, yet we must never cease to be caught up in this spiritual joy to content ourselves with God being favourable to us."[39] The congregation is to rejoice even when persecuted, hunted, and despoiled for the gospel.[40]

Today's theologian, sensitive to the gospel's call for justice, wisely cautions the preacher against encouraging the congregation to be content with oppressive circumstances.

CONTEMPORARY RUNNING COMMENTARY IN THE TRADITION REPRESENTED BY G. CAMPBELL MORGAN

G. Campbell Morgan is seldom mentioned in the homiletical literature that is popular among the clergy of the old-line denominations today. But in his lifetime (1863–1945), Morgan's expository preaching was an influential model for many clergy.[41] Using today's labels, we would call him a theological conservative.

Morgan usually takes a short text and gives it a full exposition. He may work with a few verses, or only a single verse. At times, his exposition moves word by word through the text. Morgan sets the text in its larger literary context. While he attends to the detail of the text, he draws a central point from the exposition.

Typically, Morgan begins with a few comments that set the stage for the text. He may recount the historical and literary settings of the text in a few deft sentences, or he may begin with a brief description of a contemporary need that the text and the sermon address. He often states the central point he will draw from the text; the congregation then has a framework within which to understand the details of exegesis. The heart of the sermon is exposition of the text. Frequently, the exegesis of a part of the text is followed immediately by application so that the sermon is composed of a series of movements of exegesis-application. Occasionally, the preacher presents the exegesis in a block in the first part of the sermon and then connects it in a block to the listeners in the second part. The conclusion is usually a brief appeal to the listener to take the passage to heart.

In a sermon entitled "The Burning of Heart," the announced text is Luke 24:32, but Morgan focuses on the larger narrative, which describes the encounter of two disciples with the risen Christ on the Emmaus road (Luke 24:13–35). The preacher begins, "Burning of heart. That, I take it, is the supreme need of the Church today."[42] The text can help the church's heart to burn because it is a postresurrection story, and the church is "still living in post-resurrection times."[43]

Morgan describes the travelers. He notes that even though Jesus had been crucified and buried, they continued to love him and to believe in him.

Yet, listen to them for another moment, and you will discover what they lacked. They had lost their hope, and they had lost their confidence in His ability to do what they thought he was going to do. . . . That is the picture of these men as they set their faces toward Emmaus, and it is largely the position of the Church today, as it seems to me. Personal loyalty to Jesus Christ is undoubted. It is impossible to meet with Assemblies of God's people, or to meet with individuals anywhere, without finding men who still believe in Him personally, and yet there is manifest a very widespread cooling of the Church's passion, and a dying down upon the altar of the fires which blaze in the day of the conflict which makes for victory.[44]

As the sermon develops, Morgan follows a similar pattern of exegesis and application until he concludes that the heart of the church can burn again as it becomes aware of Jesus ever with the church and as it listens to Jesus, especially as Jesus speaks through the Bible.

To be sure, G. Campbell Morgan occasionally indulges in fanciful interpretation. He can find fullness of conservative Christian doctrine in biblical passages where such orthodoxy was not envisioned by the biblical writer. But at its best, Morgan's preaching helped awaken listeners to the promises of God and to fitting human response.

The style epitomized by G. Campbell Morgan continues. We have space for only two brief illustrations. The preaching of D. Martyn Lloyd-Jones was well known in the 1960s and 1970s. As an example, we turn to Lloyd-Jones's sermons on Psalm 73. He preached eleven sermons on this psalm. He considers two or three verses in each sermon, with each sermon building on the previous ones. At the beginning of the series, he reconstructs the psalmist's situation of suffering, which has tempted the psalmist to relinquish trust in God. The sermons then trace how the psalmist moves away from this temptation.

The following excerpt demonstrates how the preacher makes a transition from one section of the psalm to another. In the previous section, Lloyd-Jones pointed out that entering the sanctuary

(the temple) and coming face to face with God is of positive benefit to the psalmist.

We must now go on, because the Psalmist's process of recovery did not stop with his going to the sanctuary. That
step is vital, and I must again emphasize it. But it is not
enough. This man went into the sanctuary of God and that
alone put his thinking in the right atmosphere. But he went
beyond that. What happened to him in the sanctuary? He
tells us. "When I thought to know this, it was too painful for
me; until I went into the sanctuary of God; then I understood
their end."[45]

The sermon explores what it means to understand God. Along
the way Lloyd-Jones sometimes extrapolates "principles" from the
text, or imports theological principles from elsewhere in the Bible
or from the larger setting of Christian doctrine within which to
understand the text. Both sets of principles are sometimes, at best,
indirectly related to the biblical text.

The preaching of Lloyd-Jones is particularly noted for the
vividness with which it moves from ancient to contemporary settings through illustration and commentary. Early in this series, to
help the congregation identify with the situation of the psalmist,
the preacher notes, "Some of you may be passing through this kind
of experience at this moment. Things may be going wrong with
you and you may be having a hard time. Blow upon blow may be
descending upon you. . . . One trouble follows another."[46]

The popular evangelical preaching of Lloyd John Ogilvie is a
contemporary example. Ogilvie frequently preaches in the mode
of running commentary. In a sermon titled "The Prodigal God"
(based on Luke 15:11–24), Ogilvie reverses the usual associations
with the word *prodigal* in connection with the parable. Taking a
cue from dictionary meanings of prodigal (extravagance, lavish,
unrestrained, copious), the preacher speaks of God's prodigality,
that is, extravagant love. Drifting in and out of allegorical interpretation, Ogilvie explains a detail of the text, and then indicates
its significance for the listeners.[47] He asks his listeners to identify with the younger child in the far country. "What would you

do in a strange city where anything was permissible because nothing mattered?"[48]

The lost son was not on the town for a lost weekend fling. He thought he had left home for good. His inheritance was tender for a new way of life. One thing mattered: what he wanted when he wanted it. After all, wasn't the money his? Wasn't he in charge of his own life now? Nobody could tell him what to do! No one dared, as long as he could pay for what he demanded.

We could leave that as an impersonal exposition of the parable if it were not for the fact that it's painfully true of life, our life. What have we done with the gift of life? Most of us are living in a frantic search for meaning, purpose, and significance. We stuff our lives with what we can taste, touch, save, or sell. The question is not "What will we do when the money runs out?" but "What can we squeeze into life and acquire before the undertaker arrives?"

The far country will take all it can get.[49]

The sermon continues alternating between historical and contemporary explanation to the predictable conclusion that the parable is the gospel in miniature—unmerited favor and love.

OTHER IMPULSES TOWARD RUNNING COMMENTARY IN CONTEMPORARY PREACHING

Contemporary preaching contains several examples of impulses toward running commentary. The following examples move toward running commentary in ways that many preachers, who have not cut their homiletical teeth on the tradition of G. Campbell Morgan, will find congenial in style, theological content, and ethical orientation. While these sermons are not all fully developed examples of running commentary, they illustrate many of its basic concerns, and they show that the genre can serve a wide variety of theological viewpoints.

Eugene Lowry speaks of "running the story."[50] The sermon follows a biblical narrative with appropriate elaboration and amplification.

The preacher creatively retells the story, explains essential elements, and helps the congregation connect it to their experience.[51]

Dennis Willis focuses on Noah's drunkenness and the display of his nakedness in Genesis 7–8.[52] Willis retells the story with imaginative annotation. He does not directly "apply" the story to the listeners, but leaves suggestions within the story that encourage the listeners to recognize themselves in it.

Willis begins by sketching Noah as one who appears to be a good man and whose sailors would sail with him anywhere. But Noah has slipped into the clutches of alcohol. In the dark tent, we encounter Noah.

Hastily moving over some objects he does not want to see, he sees there against the wall a wine skin. They all look alike. It's hard to tell. And Noah prays, "Oh God," which translated, I think, means: "Let there be enough. Just let there be enough to get me around and to get me up, to get me through. Please Lord, I don't want to get drunk. I promise, I won't get drunk. Just let there be enough to get me started, to get me around, to clean things up before they see and find out. Let there be enough."[53]

Unable to control himself, Noah drinks himself into a stupor. His son Ham sees him lying naked in his tent. Later Noah recognizes what has happened and cries out, "How did it happen? How did it come to this?"[54] Many in the congregation feel their own aches in these words that Willis puts into Noah's mouth.

In the last stages of the sermon, Willis leads the listeners to contemplate the rainbow as a sign for God: "That when God looked down he would see people through rainbows all filled with color and pretty, and God would remember that people are not made for destruction."[55] If Noah (and, by implication, Noah's descendants to this very day) could remember that fact, then perhaps Noah would have the courage to admit those aspects of his life over which he was powerless. And perhaps Noah could hold on.

If he could get that far, he wouldn't have to hold on for the rest of his life. He would only have to hold on to it for one day at a time. If he could get that far he could make a decision to turn his will and his life over to the care of a God who sees people through rainbows bright and colorful and pretty and made for creation. Made to be fed by a God who cares so much that God transforms the Divine body into bread that we can eat and into a wine that anybody can drink.[56]

Willis, like other preachers we have encountered, sometimes goes beyond the text in his imaginative retelling, especially in retrojections of Noah's thoughts and feelings. In Willis's narrative, the story is implicitly left at the level of the individual who wrestles with powerful manipulative forces, whereas Genesis views Noah in the context of the whole human community and with the structures that support life in the cosmos (Gen. 8:22). One could get the impression from Willis's sermon that the story of Noah has helped to form the basis of the contemporary psychology of addictive recovery programs.

Edmund A. Steimle was for many years professor of preaching at Union Theological Seminary in New York. Steimle's preaching often moves in the direction of running commentary. In a pithy opening for a sermon on Naaman and Elisha (2 Kings 5:1–14), Steimle reveals the main discovery of the exegesis: We do not find God as much as God finds us. As the sermon unfolds, Steimle emphasizes that God seeks us through unlikely means, especially through voices that we would not expect to bring a message from beyond.

Steimle recreates the setting and the opening scene of the text, in which a Syrian general with leprosy seeks healing. The preacher describes the general's attempt to impress God in order to get God to grant the healing. "He figured an audience with the king and some $80,000 worth of gifts was impressive enough for a man of his position and would not fail to impress this Hebrew prophet and his God."[57] Steimle then compares Naaman to us in language and imagery that is reminiscent of the 1950s when this sermon was preached.

On the face of it, it sounds ridiculous to us, of course. And yet in our expression of religion we are always tempted to behave in a manner we think befits God's station and ours.

We, too, are tempted to think that our approach to God must be "impressive," particularly if we are even a little impressed with ourselves, and we use everything from liturgies overloaded with pomp and circumstance to ecclesiastical embroidery and hocus pocus to gain this end. And I'm not forgetting the temptations that lie in wait for the clergy either, with our fondness for the prestige which is supposed to go with the office and the "pulpit tone" which always lurks around the minister's larynx.[58]

Steimle then recalls that Naaman threw a temper tantrum when the seemingly insignificant Elisha revealed God's will for healing: to wash in the unimpressive, muddy Jordan. Steimle concludes that God often speaks through unlikely people and situations. Through flashbacks, the preacher reminds the congregation that Naaman was alerted to the possibility of healing in Israel through the words of a Hebrew slave girl (also an unlikely character for divine purpose). In the last part of the sermon, Steimle gives concrete examples of how God speaks to us: through the lives and words of ordinary people, through the Bible, through the sacraments.

James L. Crenshaw, an eminent biblical scholar at Duke University, takes a commentary approach in a sermon on Revelation 21:1–5, a vision of the new heaven and the new earth. In this excerpt, Crenshaw traces the relationship between the two creations.

While the first creation had been pronounced exceptionally good by its Maker, still something was amiss. Sea, serpent, and seduction constituted a fatal flaw. Hence anticipation of a new creative act arose early.

All of us know something about the grip of the new upon our lives. We express a fascination for novelty in various ways: we celebrate New Year's Day with resolutions we know will be broken before the day is out, and we submit to baptism as a symbol of the cleansing of our sins, although we know most of them will crop up now and again. All our relationships eventually become tarnished, and we long for a clean slate. Sometimes the baggage of old memories is too much to contend with, and, sloughing off the old, we enter into new marriages, new friendships, different jobs, strange locations. Often we become addicted to the new, habitually laying ourselves open to false starts in the hope that we shall eventually discover the perfect spouse, the ideal job, just the right place. Then we risk becoming jaded, so that our fascination with and surrender to the new loses most of its appeal. Still, the text speaks with unforgettable power—it proclaims the arrival of the truly new, a universe that is pristine, pure, perfect.[59]

Crenshaw's exposition both honors the promise of the text for a new creation and, at the same time, exposes the human inclination, so characteristic of life in the old earth, to misuse the gift of the promise of the new.

These snapshots from the family album do not tell the whole story of preaching as running commentary. But they reveal that this type of preaching has played significant roles in the preaching and teaching of Judaism and Christianity. (Indeed, for some, these pictures might even function as dynamite to clear a homestead for preaching and teaching in the style of running commentary.) We may chuckle at some of the eisegesis of the Qumranians or Origen or G. Campbell Morgan. But lest we become too satisfied with our interpretive perspectives, we need to remember that each generation has found its predecessors wanting in one way or another. Successive generations likely will look upon aspects of our exegesis and theology with bemusement. In the midst of the finitude that is part of life this side of the eschaton, preaching as running commentary has shown uncommon resilience to adapt to new eras and new visions in biblical interpretation and Christian doctrine. Today's preacher who finds promise in this genre is called to bring the best of exegetical, theological, hermeneutical, aesthetic, and pastoral discernment to the sermon.

3

Preparing the
Verse by Verse Sermon

Tom Boomershine, a leader in the biblical storytelling movement, tells the story of flying to Israel in the company of a group of African American preachers. During their journey, he noticed that they were engaging in lively give-and-take with each other. Tom began to listen. In a short time, he found himself engrossed in some of the most exciting sermon preparation he had ever experienced. On a plane, high above the Atlantic Ocean, they were moving through a passage aloud in a group—exploring words, sharing information, asking questions, identifying what they found fascinating and challenging, bantering with the text and with each other, listening to the passage from different perspectives in the text, laughing, and always moving deeper and deeper into engagement with the text.

This kind of conversation with a passage from the Bible, and with the community in which the sermon will come to life, is the essence of preparation for verse by verse preaching. The preacher seeks to enter the world of the text and to help the congregation enter that world too. As in the tradition of Jewish midrash, the preacher and congregation aim to become immersed in the details and depths of the text. They are alert to sparks of insight, to aspects of the text that clarify, empower, puzzle, challenge, disturb, and even offend. The verse by verse format encourages a sensitive preacher to acknowledge such discoveries in the process of preparation, and to bring them into the sermon itself. While the sermon typically comes to a resolution, an occasional sermon (taking its cue from the content of the biblical text or from uncertainties that arise in connection with its theology or significance for the congregation) may leave the congregation hanging, with further work to do.

In verse by verse preaching, as in midrash, the text is a conversation partner. Some preachers invite members of the congregation into sermon preparation, usually through a group that meets in advance of the sermon to help the preacher consider the text from their perspective.[1] This group is sometimes called a *feedforward* group because they help feed the sermon as it is moving forward to the pulpit. The verse by verse approach provides a format that a preacher could easily use to structure such a conversation. Other essential dialogue partners include helps for interpreting the Bible (e.g., commentaries, Bible dictionaries, concordances, and studies of particular biblical passages or themes), volumes of historical and systematic theology, the arts, and other resources that help preachers interpret the Bible for the living community today. These materials often bring to our attention characteristics of the biblical literature that open to us a broader understanding of the passage in its historical, literary, theological, and ecclesiological settings.

Preparing the verse by verse sermon is not fundamentally different from preparing any sermon that centers on the exposition of a biblical text. The preacher needs to give careful attention both to the trees and to the forest. The verse by verse approach brings with it the danger that the preacher will so focus on the trees that both pastor and congregation lose sight of the forest within which the text resides. The preacher needs to find a place to stand from which to view the woods as a whole and how the forest fits into the larger landscape. We stress that preachers need to avoid the temptation to work so much on the details of the text that they give insufficient attention to more comprehensive questions, especially larger questions of theological meaning.

Consequently, in this chapter we consider dimensions of sermon preparation that are important for verse by verse preaching. After a brief review of essential steps in exegesis that highlights aspects that are important for preparing this kind of sermon, we examine the interpretation of several different forms (genres) of biblical texts with an eye toward considerations that the preacher may want to take into account in the verse by verse sermon. We look at an epiphany story (the transfiguration), a pronouncement story (Mary and Martha), an apocalyptic vision (the first four trumpets from the book of Revelation), an etiology (Jacob's ladder), a parable (the sower and the soils). In chapter 4, we offer sermons on these texts.

A REVIEW OF EXEGETICAL METHOD
AND THE VERSE BY VERSE SERMON

The following review of basic exegetical method is presented in thirteen sequential steps. Seasoned preachers develop their own patterns of engaging a text that may, or may not, follow this (or any other) sequence.[2] The ministers on the airplane, whom we described at the beginning of this chapter, did not follow this series of steps. One of us attended a seminar in Germany at which a major professor of New Testament outlined a linear progression in exegesis, whereupon one of this professor's students responded, "I don't follow these steps. I just dive in and swim." However, regardless of the preacher's pattern of engaging the text in the preparation of the sermon, most preachers need to get around to these concerns by the time they step into the pulpit in order to interact with the text at the depth necessary for interpreting it with integrity in the Christian community.

We recognize that many parish needs compete with the pastor's need to interact in a significant way with the Bible. Pastors need to find the optimum time of the day and week for conversation with the Bible and their optimum style of doing so, and dedicate these times and approaches to sermon preparation. We offer some suggestions: (a) Pastors can look for opportunities early in the process of preparation for introducing the text to members of the congregation and making note of their feedback. For example, the minister might make such use of the text when asked to lead midweek devotions in a meeting, or as part of a weekly Bible study group. (b) A pastor might preach a series of sermons on a single book of the Bible. Steps 2 and 6 (below) will provide essential background information that carries from week to week. (c) Pastors need to gather commentaries that provide a wide range of interpretive methodologies. We hope that they do not simply use commentaries as sources of data, but that they regard them as conversation partners to help with their fresh interpretive thinking. (d) Pastors can take advantage of continuing education events and clergy colleague groups that provide up-to-date perspectives on interpreting and preaching on books of the Bible. (e) We recommend that pastors practice biblical exegesis every day in the same way that persons practice musical instruments or sports. Practice typically increases competence. Practice creates conditions under which fresh insight can break forth. Perhaps in a given week, a minister cannot give full attention to one or more of the steps. However, when working with the same biblical book over a period of time, a preacher can accumulate a reservoir of perspectives that can tide the preacher over from one week to another.

Essential Steps

1. Determine meaningful limits for the passage. The first rule of exegesis is to make sure that the passage begins and ends at natural points so that the sermon deals with a meaningful unit of material. Additionally, the preacher needs to focus on a text that can be discussed adequately in the time available for the sermon. Of course, there are no hard and fast rules for determining the length of a text that a preacher can handle in a verse by verse sermon. In a congregation in which a sermon lasts about twenty minutes, we find that ten to twenty verses is usually about right. In congregations in which the sermon is shorter, shorter passages are often more satisfactory, while a congregation socialized for a forty-minute sermon can afford the preacher a longer passage.

2. Insofar as possible, identify the historical setting of the passage and the situation to which the passage was written. Such knowledge can often help preachers feel the force of a passage that they might otherwise miss. This exercise often requires some subtlety on the part of the preacher in distinguishing various levels of historical situation. For instance, the story of the exodus from Egypt is told as if the historical situation is slavery and deliverance from Egypt. However, the book of Exodus was given much of its present form around the time of the exile in Babylonia. The preacher needs to know which level of the historical setting is informing the sermon.[3] The verse by verse preacher will usually want to help the congregation learn this context and how such knowledge can help in interpreting the passage. We qualify this step with the phrase "insofar as possible" because we cannot always reconstruct the historical setting of a passage with confidence.

3. Discern the form (genre) of the passage and its intention. Literary criticism and rhetorical criticism have taught us that most biblical texts are examples of particular forms or genres (e.g., parable, miracle story, saga, community lament) that were well known in antiquity. Each example of a genre had a particular purpose in the light of its use in the document in which it is found. The verse by verse expository preacher needs to help the community name this genre and its purpose in its present literary and historical context.

4. Determine the movement of the passage and the units of the text that will be the subjects of the exposition in the sermon. Literary and rhetorical critics call the preacher to discern the internal movement of the passage. How does the text achieve its purpose? This discovery may cause the preacher to realize that the sermon should follow the movement of the text, but in a way other than verse by verse. The units of meaning, or sense units, in the passage may not fall neatly along verse lines, but may be multiple verses, or may be as brief as parts of verses. In these cases, the preacher can help the congregation realize that the traditional versification actually obscures the natural subdivisions of meaning in the text. We find it helpful to make a list of the divisions in the text that will form the groupings of material in the exposition in the sermon. For example, the movement of a passage might fall into the following sense units: (a) vv. 1–2, (b) v. 3, (c) vv. 4–5a, (d) v. 5b, (e) vv. 6–8. The structure of the sermon would correspond to these five bodies of material.

This aspect of analysis also includes *noting the literary context of the passage.* Obviously, the literary context includes the material that precedes and follows the text. How does the immediate placement of the text affect our hearing of it? Literary context also includes the placement of the individual passage in the larger movement of the book (or body of literature) in which it is found. A passage may contain words, phrases, images, or ideas that connect it to other passages or even themes in the book. Some literary contexts extend beyond a single book to encompass a body of literature (e.g., the Pentateuch, the letters of Paul).

5. *Work through the text unit by unit, and word by word, exploring the meaning(s) of its constituent parts.* This is the heart of exegesis. With the help of a concordance, commentaries, Bible dictionaries, special studies, and other interpretive helps, the preacher determines the resonance of each word of the text in conjunction with other words and associations in the text and in the larger worlds of the Bible and the ancient Near East. The preacher seeks to determine how a word, in interplay with other words in the text, would have been heard by persons in antiquity. The pastor will nearly always turn up more material than can be used in any single sermon, and, consequently, will need to distinguish between those things that are essential for the congregation to hear, and those things that are enriching but can wait for another sermon. Two words of caution are in order. First, a preacher needs to avoid making the sermon nothing more than a series of word studies. That approach does violence to the literary and theological integrity of the passage. Moreover, congregations often find it boring. Second, preachers need to avoid thinking that a generic definition of a word in a Bible dictionary or other scholarly source is the full understanding of the word. Words in texts take on particular meanings because of the part that they play in the world of the text.

6. *Summarize the meanings of the passage in its historical and literary contexts.* We emphasize "meanings" because scholars are more and more aware of the multivalence of passages. Multivalence has a double frame of reference: First, a passage has more meaning than can be satisfactorily expressed in a single formulation. Second, the location of the interpreter (theologically, ecclesiologically, historically, socially, economically, politically, by race and gender, etc.) affects what he or she is prepared to hear and not to hear in a passage. Given these relativities, a preacher may find it helpful to summarize the meanings of a passage that come to her or him in the light of the passage's historical and literary settings as a way of

consolidating what she or he has discovered in preparation for the next phases of sermon preparation.

7. *Identify the theological claims of the passage.* Each passage contains claims that it asks us to accept as true concerning God, the world, and our response. The preacher needs to identify these claims in order to bring them into sharp relief and to help determine our hermeneutical relationship with them.

8. *Analyze the claims of the passage theologically.* In order to determine the hermeneutical relationship between the congregation and the passage, the preacher needs to analyze the claims of the passage theologically (this relationship is discussed in connection with step 9 below). Three questions are paramount here. First, are the claims of the passage appropriate to (consistent with) the gospel?[4] We take the gospel to be the news, confirmed through Jesus Christ, of God's unconditional love for each and all, and God's irrepressible will for justice for each and all.

Second, is the text intelligible to the congregation? Does it make sense? Intelligibility has three levels. (a) Are the claims of the text *clear?* Can we understand them? Sometimes the preacher needs to help the congregation bring the claims of the text into focus. (b) Are the claims of the text *coherent* with other things that Christians believe and do? When the claims of a text contradict other things that Christians believe and do, the preacher needs to help the congregation ask whether the problem is in the church's misperception and misbehavior, or in some misrepresentation within the text itself. (c) Are the claims of the text *believable* given the ways in which we understand the world today? Admittedly, this question is problematic and open to wide interpretation. Nonetheless, the preacher seeks, in the language of theologian David Kelsey, to determine whether the claims of the text are "seriously imaginable,"[5] that is, that we can believe that the claims of the text can really be true and are not merely fantasy.

Third, does the text call for the moral treatment of all in its world? That is, does the text call for all persons to be treated as unconditionally loved by God, and with justice? In the verse by verse sermon, the preacher can choose whether to bring this analysis into the consciousness of the congregation as a part of the exposition of the text's details, or as a distinct part of the sermon.

9. Determine the hermeneutical relationship between the text and the congregation. Based on the theological analysis of the claims of the passage, the preacher determines the hermeneutical relationship with the congregation. Typically this relationship will move in one of three directions:

First, when the claims of the text are appropriate to the gospel, intelligible, and morally plausible, the preacher can help the congregation determine how the text assures, confirms, enlarges, or challenges the congregation. A text may assure a congregation of something that it needs to know and that builds it up. A text may confirm what the congregation already believes. It may ask the congregation to envision God or its mission in larger terms. It may challenge a congregation to rediscover forgotten beliefs, or it may ask the congregation to admit that aspects of its belief and behavior need correction.

Second, when some aspect of the text is unintelligible, or inappropriate to the gospel, the preacher needs to help the congregation clarify those parts that are authoritative and those parts that are not. For instance, many texts in the four Gospels portray the Jewish community in caricature for the purpose of downgrading Judaism and justifying the growing divide between the church and the synagogue in the first century C.E. While this development is understandable, it is inappropriate to the gospel because it denies God's unconditional love to Jewish people, and it does not seek justice for them. The preacher can help the congregation see that the underlying claim of many of these texts (that God's liberating love is at work in the world through Jesus Christ) is true without portraying the Jewish community in caricature. To take another example, a miracle story may report that a natural phenomenon is immediately responsive to the divine command. While such one-to-one correlation between natural phenomena and divine command is not typical of the view of the world shared by many people today, the preacher can still use the text as an analogy for identifying God's restorative purposes in the world today.

Third, the claims of a very few texts are so deeply inappropriate to the gospel, unintelligible, and morally implausible, that the preacher must speak against them. For instance, Psalm 58 prays, "Let them [my enemies] vanish like water that runs away. . . . Let them be like . . . the untimely birth that never sees the sun" (vv. 7, 9). Such texts perform a positive role in the church by forcing the church to think clearly about what it truly believes about God. As we pointed out in the first chapter, the verse by verse sermon provides the preacher with an ideal venue for pointing out the theological and moral problems with a text. Further, in this case, the sermon needs to be more than a critique of the text. After exposing the inadequacies of a text, the sermon can become an occasion for encountering the gospel.

10. Designate what you hope will happen in the congregation as a result of participating in the sermon. One of the dangers of the verse by verse sermon is that it will degenerate into a series of comments about the text that never bring the text as a whole into view. Pastors can work against this possibility by being clear about what they hope will happen in the community. What does the pastor hope the congregation will think? What does the pastor hope the congregation will feel? How does the pastor hope the congregation's behavior will be affected? The preacher then can shape the exposition of the text so that it moves toward these goals. Of course, an experienced preacher knows that sermons often turn out very differently than expected because of the situation of the congregation, the work of the Holy Spirit, and other factors beyond the cognizance and control of the preacher.

11. Plan the movement of the sermon using the sense units as the basic outline of the sermon and deciding which ones to emphasize and which can be discussed in a more cursory fashion. In the verse by verse sermon, the movement of the passage determines the movement of the sermon. However, given the limitations of time, and the fact that not all material in a text is equally important, a preacher may need to give more time to the parts of the text that are pivotal for the sermon and less time to parts of the text that are not as significant.

12. Help the congregation make connections between the world of the text and their own world. The verse by verse preacher can make these connections in one of two ways. We illustrate both of these patterns in the sermons in chapter 4.

First, as a general rule, we think it preferable to unfold the contemporary significance of the text with the exposition. As soon as a preacher offers the exegesis of a sense unit, the preacher would then help the congregation make a positive connection to their world. Frequently the preacher can help the congregation make an analogy between the text and their setting by asking the question, "Who or what in our world is similar to the setting/character/action in this sense unit of the text?"[6] The sermon then follows the movement of the text. This approach suggests the interpenetration of the text and our setting. When preaching against a text, of course, a preacher can point out the theological and moral improprieties of the text.

Second, the preacher may also wait until the end of the sermon to draw out the implications of the exposition for today's world. The preacher first renders the verse by verse exposition (in a block of material), and then asks the question, "What does this exposition have to do with us?" The response to the question is a second block of material. While this approach can be very clear, it can also lead to the subtle bifurcation between the worlds of the Bible and today. It can also be tedious for the listeners, especially when the exposition is dry and hard to follow.

13. As an aid to preparation, we recommend that the preacher make a chart that maps the flow of the sermon. We provide illustrations of such flowcharts at the beginning of the sermons in chapter 4. A flowchart helps the preacher get an overview of the movement of the sermon, its points of contact with the congregation, and its proportions.

INTERPRETING GENRES OF TEXT

As we discuss the representative texts mentioned previously, we cannot engage in a full-scale exegesis of each one. We do, however, call attention to things that the verse by verse preacher can take into account in the preparation of the sermon. In order to help show that the verse by verse approach can be used with the broad spectrum of biblical literature, we discuss passages from a wide variety of genres.

THE TRANSFIGURATION OF JESUS:
AN EPIPHANY STORY

We focus on the transfiguration of Jesus in Luke 9:28–36, an obviously meaningful unit. The Gospel of Luke and the book of Acts were written by the same author, tell a single narrative, and presuppose the same historical setting. The interpretive context is thus Luke-Acts and its various worlds (historical, literary, theological). The historical setting of Luke-Acts is important for understanding the transfiguration. These two volumes were written to a congregation (or group of congregations) in an undisclosed location outside of Palestine about 80–90 C.E. In its formative years, the church had been a part of traditional Judaism. In fact, some scholars refer to the earliest Christian community as a group of Christian Jews. However, the Gentile mission created tension between the traditional synagogue and the Christian community. When Luke writes, the distance between the two communities is growing and becoming more painful. Some members of the church may have been subject to synagogue legal proceedings and discipline. Families and friendships were breaking up. How should the church understand its relationship to Jewish tradition? Ironically, like some other Jewish communities, the church was in danger of losing its distinctive identity as a people of the God of Israel. The church was also in danger of so absorbing Hellenistic culture that it could lose this same identity. The church was in a crisis of identity. The transfiguration speaks directly to this concern.

The overarching literary theme of Luke-Acts is that God is manifesting the divine rule through the ministry of Jesus Christ. The divine rule (reign of God, rule of God, dominion of God, holy commonwealth of God) is that time when all relationships conform in every way to God's purposes. God's love and justice permeate all situations. In Luke-Acts this motif has a strong apocalyptic character that assumes that history is divided into two ages—a present broken age and the coming reign of God. Through

Christ, God is invading the old age and demonstrating the new. The complete transformation from old to new will be completed when Jesus returns in glory. In the meantime, the church is to continue to witness to this age. As noted in the word by word exegesis below, the witness to the new world often involves suffering. The Gentile mission is a part of the eschatological reunion of the scattered peoples of the world.

While many kinds of literature in the Bible are relatively easy to categorize (e.g., saga, Gospel, proverb, wisdom saying, parable, miracle story), scholars have had difficulty identifying the specific literary genre of the transfiguration. We think that *epiphany story* best names this short narrative.[7] The Greek root of the word *epiphany* means "to show forth." An epiphany story reveals, or shows forth, the identity of the central character and the community that centers on that character. However, an epiphany text does not offer the listeners a propositional summary of the identity of the main character. It creates a narrative world. The listeners discover the identity of the main character by entering into the narrative and imaginatively experiencing the story world. Luke's listeners journey with Jesus and the disciples to the mountaintop. By entering into the narrative world, the identity of Jesus is revealed, as are some of its implications for Luke's community in crisis.

The movement of the story is quite simple. The disciples go with Jesus up the mountain to its top, where Jesus is transfigured. This metamorphosis reveals something significant about Jesus. The disciples respond inappropriately. The passage climaxes in a saying of Jesus directed immediately to the disciples, but more generally to the listener of Luke's Gospel. The sense units in this story fall roughly along the lines of the verses, although some verses must be combined in single units of meaning. The sense units can form the movement of the sermon: v. 28 (the setting); vv. 29–31 (the transfiguration itself: the experience of the transcendent realm of God); vv. 32–33 (the response of the disciples); vv. 34–36 (the cloud and the voice); v. 37 (the ending). The immediate literary context is important for interpreting the story: the revelation of suffering as the way of messiahship and discipleship (Luke 9:18–27). The theme of suffering as a part of the witness of Jesus and the early church to the manifestation of the rule of God permeates the rest of the Gospel and Acts.

We have space to mention only the highlights of working through the text word by word. The setting (in prayer on a mountain) clues us to expect a revelatory event (v. 28). Jesus' body is transformed into the kind of body that people will have in the reign of God. This change assures the disciples (and the listeners) that Jesus is the agent through whom God is manifesting afresh the new world, and it demonstrates the character of the transformation. Moses and Elijah appear beside Jesus to show that the ministry of Jesus and the church are in continuity with the Jewish tradition. Jesus' "departure" in Jerusalem will be a part of this process. In Greek, the term *departure* is *exodos*, from which we get our word *exodus*, thus calling to mind the exodus of the children of Israel from Egypt as a framework within which to understand the death of Jesus.

The disciples respond by wanting to build three dwellings (vv. 32–33). The Greek word rendered "dwellings" can also be translated "tents." If so, the latter refers to the Feast of Booths (tents). The Jewish community probably observed the Feast of Booths by temporarily living in tents. The Feast of Booths honored the time that God dwelled (tented) with Israel while they were in the wilderness after the exodus from Egypt. This Feast came to symbolize the eschatological world when God would dwell fully and perpetually with the community (see Zech. 14:16 when the Feast of Booths is celebrated in Jerusalem). In this latter sense, the phrase "not knowing what he said" would better be rendered, "although he did not know what he was saying." Peter said more than he knew, for he recognized the eschatological character of the event. However, the mountaintop is not the top on which to set up the eschatological tents, for the eschatological event will not be complete until Jesus returns.

The cloud betokens the divine presence (vv. 34–36). The voice echoes God's words at the baptism, and invokes the memory of Isaiah 42:1, the beginning of the first of Isaiah's Servant Songs. The Servant Songs in Isaiah assert that the servant (Israel) will be a light to the nations. To be a light is to witness to God's love and justice. However, suffering is the means whereby that witness comes to expression (Isa. 52:13–53:12). The voice may also echo Psalm 2:7, a coronation passage sung on the day that the king was anointed as ruler of Israel, and was given the title, son of God. The principal work of the king was to mediate justice in the community. The ministry of Jesus and the church extend these emphases from Judaism into the Gentile world. The expression "Listen to him!" reminds the listener to pay attention to what Jesus has just said (namely, that messiahship and discipleship follow the tradition of redemptive suffering exemplified by Isaiah [Luke 9:18–27]), and to pay attention to all that Jesus says, for Jesus speaks under the authority of the divine.

From a dramatic standpoint the ending (v. 37) is anticlimactic. However, its narrative function is to prompt the listener to ponder the story of what has happened on the mountain, and to remember what Jesus has said. The sermon could end similarly.

By way of summary, we note that the transfiguration is a taste of the glory of the eschatological world. However, the transformation of the world involves suffering witness on the part of Jesus, the disciples, and the subsequent church. The story of the transfiguration is designed to strengthen Jesus and the church as they face difficulty, persecution, even rejection. These are the primary theological claims of the story.

The text is certainly appropriate to the gospel as it anticipates the transformation of the world into a place in which all know God's unconditional love and all live in justice. The claims of the text are also intelligible. We can understand them. They cohere with other things that Christians believe and do. While the event of the transfiguration is outside of our experience, the story is a powerful symbol of divine presence becoming manifest in our midst. Indeed, the story is a lens through which to recognize moments in our world in which we see people and situations transfigured, that is, anticipating the world that is to come. The claims of the text are also morally plausible, for the text does not deny God's love or justice.

Since the claims of the text are appropriate to the gospel, intelligible, and morally plausible, the congregation is in the first hermeneutical relationship with the passage (see step 9, above). The preacher needs to determine how the text confirms, enlarges, or challenges the congregation. In the sermon on this text in chapter 4, the preacher uses the story of the transfiguration to help enlarge and focus the congregation's understanding of the divine presence. In particular, the preacher asks, "Figuratively speaking, how do we go to the mountaintop? How do we experience God's strengthening presence in the face of challenges to our attempts to witness to the gospel?" A flowchart precedes the sermon showing the sense units of the text and their relationship to the points of hermeneutical contact with the congregation.

MARY AND MARTHA: A PRONOUNCEMENT STORY

Luke 10:38–42, the story of Jesus in the home of Mary and Martha, is a passage whose boundaries are neatly demarcated. While we discussed the historical context of Luke-Acts in connection with the transfiguration (above), we did not mention two aspects of that setting that are important for understanding the story of Mary and Martha. The first is a crisis of authority in the particular church to which Luke-Acts was written. What are the sources from the past and present that are authoritative in the community? Who are reliable interpreters of past and present? Luke-Acts presumes that the Septuagint (the Greek translation of the Hebrew Bible) is the primary authority from the past, and that Jesus, empowered by the Holy Spirit, is its primary interpreter. Jesus establishes the apostles (the Twelve, who are also empowered by the Spirit) as authorities. Their authority is demonstrated in Acts. In Acts, the apostles, in cooperation with the Holy Spirit, authorize Paul to undertake the Gentile mission. The community can regard leaders as authoritative when it follows the trajectory of interpretation set in motion by Jesus and the Twelve as depicted in Luke-Acts.

The second crisis is the place and role of women in the church. Do women have full standing in the Christian community? Can women serve as teachers and in other positions of leadership? As is well known, in the patriarchal historical period in which Luke-

Acts was written, social roles were organized in pyramid fashion with some persons and roles taking precedence over others. Men had a higher place on the pyramid than women. The interpreter needs to handle this motif with delicacy. On the one hand, women did not have as many opportunities as men to own property and run businesses, to have their own homes, or otherwise to be self-determining. In Jewish tradition, this secondary status was justified (in part) by the story of the Fall in Genesis 3. God placed women under a curse. On the other hand, interpreters sometimes speak of the situation of women in the first century C.E. in caricature, as if women were nothing more than chattel that could be manipulated at will by men. In many communities in the world of the first century (including many in Judaism) women had increasing freedoms. However, the apocalyptic tradition anticipated the day, in the reign of God, when the curse on women would be altogether removed, and women would be restored to the egalitarian partnership with men that is remembered from Genesis 1 and 2.

The story of Mary and Martha is a pronouncement story. As its name implies, the pronouncement story is a narrative that highlights a pronouncement of Jesus. The pronouncement is an authoritative statement. While the pronouncement is the climax of the storyline within the narrative, it is also directed toward those who are listening to the story. The pronouncement is designed to help clear up ambiguities in a community's setting and to offer a clear perspective by which to interpret aspects of the community's life. The movement of the story of Mary and Martha falls into sense units that follow this pattern and that become the structure of the sermon that follows: the setting (v. 38), the differing activities of Mary and Martha (vv. 39–40), the pronouncement of Jesus (vv. 41–42).

The wider literary setting of the story of Mary and Martha is the journey of Jesus and the disciples from Galilee to Jerusalem (Luke 9:51–19:27), where the definitive revelation of Jesus' ministry will take place through the cross, resurrection, and ascension. The journey is itself a model for the life of discipleship and Christian community—discipleship is a journey through life with Jesus. In Acts the church is even called "the Way." The story of Mary and

Martha partakes of the essential purpose of this part of the Gospel of Luke: to reveal essential qualities of the way of discipleship.

The immediate literary context is also illuminating. Just after beginning the journey to Jerusalem, Jesus sends seventy witnesses on a mission to witness to the rule of God (10:1–24). When they return, Jesus tells the parable of the Good Samaritan in response to the question, "Who is my neighbor?" Given the preceding events in the Gospel, the listener understands the question to include, "What are the boundaries of those to whom we take the news of the rule of God? And what are the limits of those who can carry the news?" The answer: the news of the rule of God goes as far as those who are as good as dead (represented by the person in the ditch) and it can be carried by all, even those from whom we have been alienated (represented by the Samaritan). The story confirms that women are also recipients of the benefits of the rule of God, and they can be prepared to become its agents.

Digging through the text word by word, we notice that the story is directly opened as a window on the life of discipleship—"Now as they went on their way." In that world, women were typically identified by reference to the males with whom they were in relationship (e.g., father, husband, brother). Relatively few women lived in their own homes. Yet Martha and Mary are identified in their own right, without reference to males. The text implies that they are in their own house.

When Martha welcomes Jesus into the home, she implicitly agrees to provide typical Middle Eastern hospitality for a guest: washing the feet, preparing a meal, engaging in other acts to help the guest feel at ease. These actions are typically performed by women, and Martha sets about them.

Mary, however, sits at Jesus' feet and listens to him. While this Mary is a different person from the Mary of Jesus' birth, the listener remembers that the first Mary is a model believer in the Gospel of Luke and imports that association to this Mary. The posture of sitting at Jesus' feet calls to mind rabbinical custom. The rabbi sat when giving authoritative teaching, and disciples sat at that rabbi's feet. The casual use of the word "listening" recalls the transfiguration and the admonition that Jesus' disciples are to listen to him. Throughout the Gospel, Jesus teaches the apostles and the wider circle of disciples to prepare them to become a community of witness to the reign of God. In this scene Jesus is teaching Mary, a self-determining woman, for those purposes.

Martha is performing the traditional woman's role by herself, and she implores the visiting rabbi to send Mary to tend to those tasks as well. Jesus' pronouncement offers the authoritative interpretation: Mary has chosen wisely to sit at Jesus' feet. In the book of Acts, we learn that Priscilla is an authoritative teacher (Acts 18:24–28). Luke is acknowledging that women not only have full access to sacred tradition, but that they can be leaders in Christian community. In order to be able to lead, they (like men) must have opportunities to listen.

Luke does not hereby abolish all practice of hospitality. Later in the Gospel, Jesus receives traditional hospitality from others. The members of the early church are hospitable. The hospitality of others makes possible Paul's missionary journeys. Hospitality can be practiced in the service of the divine rule. Martha's problem is that she is "distracted" and "worried." These terms characterize life in the old age (note particularly "worry," *merimnao, merimna,* in Luke 12:11, 22, 25, 26; 21:34). Martha's hospitality attempts to reproduce patterns of feeling and behavior that were characteristic of the old world, but that are now obviated by the presence of the reign of God through Jesus.

To summarize, we can say that Martha's anxious, distracted behavior represents the situation of women in the old age, whereas Mary signals the renewed situation of women in the restoration of relationship that is a part of the rule of God. Luke asserts that women have full access to the authoritative teaching of the community, and can become authoritative teachers and leaders in the community.

These claims are self-evidently appropriate to a Gospel that announces God's unconditional love and God's call for justice. They are intelligible in that we can easily understand them, they are logically consistent with other things that Christians should believe and do, and they cohere with the ways in which we can experience the role and place of women in the world today. This story is morally plausible. Indeed, to women and others in situations in which they are arbitrarily restricted or repressed, this story comes as a message of liberation.

The hermeneutical relationship between the story and the congregation is the first one that we mentioned in step 9, above. When the claims of the text are appropriate to the gospel, intelligible, and morally plausible, the preacher can help the congregation determine how the text confirms, enlarges, or challenges the congregation. The story of Mary and Martha may confirm what the congregation already believes about the place and possibilities for women in Christian community. It may ask the congregation to envision a larger place for women in its life. It may challenge a congregation to admit that it has been complicit in relegating women to the secondary roles characteristic of the old age. In the sermon in chapter 4, the preacher moves through the story to help us recognize that the gracious claim and presence of Jesus relieve us—men as well as women—of anxiety and distraction, and set us free to listen and to witness. A flowchart comes before the sermon and shows the sense units of the text and their relationship to the points of hermeneutical contact with the congregation.

THE FOUR TRUMPETS: APOCALYPTIC VISION

Revelation 8:6–12, with its vision of the four trumpets, is a satisfactory segment of scripture for interpretation. The four trumpets do form a discrete group (like the four seals of 6:1–8). However, this passage is only part of a larger vision of seven trumpets (Rev. 8:2–11:19). While the preacher can offer a meaningful interpretation of Revelation 8:6–12 as a discrete unit, the fuller literary context is the complete vision. The extended passage, however, is too long for close exposition in a single verse by verse sermon. In order to converse with the congregation about the complete vision, a pastor might preach a series of sermons on all seven trumpets, or might preach a sermon that relies heavily on summarizing the various parts of the vision.

The historical setting of Revelation is important to the verse by verse preacher. Most scholars agree that the book of Revelation was written for a group of churches in Asia Minor in 90–96 C.E. The last half of the first century C.E. was a chaotic time in the Roman Empire, marked by rebellion and military conflict and by dramatic natural disaster (Mount Vesuvius erupted in 79 C.E., burying the city of Pompeii). Many people were in poverty. Many religious and philosophical movements thrived as people sought to find security in the midst of social crisis.

The congregations to whom the book of Revelation was directed were either in the midst of persecution or afraid that persecution was imminent. John, the early Christian prophet who received this revelation, was in political incarceration on the island of Patmos "because of the word of God and the testimony of Jesus." We do not have definitive evidence to explain why he was imprisoned. We do know that Domitian, the emperor at the time John wrote, was widely regarded as divine. Many scholars think that emperor worship, required for full participation in Roman life, required a confession, "Caesar is Lord." To Christians, such a viewpoint was idolatrous. For Christians, Jesus is Lord. Presumably, John and many other Christians would not pledge allegiance to the Roman state by confessing the sovereignty of Caesar, and were harassed as a result.

As an apocalyptic theologian, John regards the history of the world as divided into two eras: this decaying, sinful age that will pass away, and a coming new world in which all things will conform to God's purposes. In a dramatic historical cataclysm, God will destroy the old world and its rulers, and will install the new world. For John, the Roman world is the epitome of the old order. Indeed, invoking one of the most visceral images from the prophetic tradition, the book of Revelation refers to Rome as the great whore of Babylon. God will dismantle and condemn it, and replace it with a new social order. According to the book of Revelation, the suffering of the world, and particularly the suffering of the Christian community, is part of the increasing tension in history that is expected prior to the apocalyptic cataclysm.

John receives an apocalypse, a series of visions from God (mediated through Jesus Christ and an angel) to interpret the situation of the wider world and of the church. The purpose of an apocalypse is

to offer the community hope and encouragement in the midst of difficulty by identifying those forces and behaviors in the world that are
of God, and those that are opposed to God. The apocalypse is an interpretive guide in how to understand events that are taking place so
that the community will not be awash in uncertainty and misperception. The basic theological conviction of apocalyptic literature is
that God reigns. God is in control of history and is permitting the
forces of evil to assert themselves, because such assertion is self-
destructive. As the sermon based on this text shows in chapter 4,
apocalyptic literature contains a strong component of social criticism
in that it names and critiques the present social trends on the basis
of the vision of God's transcendent rule, especially God's sovereignty
and God's will for justice.

Apocalypses comprise different genres (e.g., letter, angelic discourse, testament). Revelation 8:6–12 is a symbolic vision. In a
symbolic vision, the writer uses symbols from the First Testament
and other Jewish literature in order to make sense of the present
situation of the world. The listener recognizes the meaning(s) of
the symbol in its First Testament historical and literary contexts,
and uses those meanings as a lens through which to interpret
contemporary situations. The apocalyptic writers frequently use
elements of the exodus from Egypt as a paradigm by which to understand the time of the later community; they also use images of
judgment and redemption from the prophets. In the later period,
God is moving toward a cosmic exodus event, a universal judgment
and restoration. Although apocalyptic symbolic expression seems
quite strange to many people living in the twenty-first century, it
was commonplace to Christians in the first century, and they could
easily understand it. The verse by verse preacher needs to explain
such symbolism carefully in its settings in the First Testament and
in the apocalyptic text. The preacher then needs to ask, "Does this
symbolism help the Christian community today interpret our
world?"

The literary context is useful to the verse by verse preacher.
Revelation 4:1–5:14 asserts the sovereignty of God and reminds
the reader that all things in history take place either by God's direct command or by God's permission. Therefore, the community

can live in confidence, knowing that the events that are subsequently described (no matter how fearful or violent) are under God's control. Revelation 6:1–8:1, the vision of the opening of the seven seals, reveals God's condemnation of many aspects of the Roman world. The idolatry, violence, and natural disasters that are taking place are a part of God's judgment. The time of complete condemnation and collapse is not yet—Death and Hades are given authority over only a fourth of the earth. However, history is moving toward the final end of the reign of evil. The Christian community need not fear, for 144,000 (a symbolic number meaning all who are in the community of the faithful) will be saved.

Revelation 8:2 initiates the vision of seven trumpets. The trumpets refer to many events that are similar to those mentioned in the seven seals. However, the extent of destruction now covers one-third of the earth. Expressions of evil, and the force of divine judgment, are intensified. History is moving closer toward the apocalyptic cataclysm.

Revelation 8:6–12 provides the preacher with a breakdown of units of meaning: the symbolism of the trumpet itself (v. 6), the blowing of the first trumpet (v. 7), the blowing of the second trumpet (vv. 8–9), the blowing of the third trumpet (vv. 10–11), the blowing of the fourth trumpet (vv. 12). Verse 13 functions more as an introduction to the next three trumpet blasts (9:1ff.), and, consequently, should be discussed in the latter context. In the sermon on this passage in chapter 4, the preacher generally follows this structure, but adjusts it slightly in order to compress the discussion of the second and third trumpets into a single section of the sermon because of similarities of imagery in those trumpet blasts.

When interpreting apocalyptic literature, it is especially important for the preacher to proceed image by image because the meaning(s) of apocalyptic visions result from the accumulated meaning(s) of the separate images. The trumpet is an instrument that, in Jewish tradition, frequently signals that an action of God is taking place. The trumpet is sometimes specifically associated with divine judgment, as it is here. The trumpet calls the community to repent in the face of judgment. Number symbolism is important in apocalyptic literature; the number seven represents completeness.

When the seven trumpets are completed, the reader knows that a phase of the history of the world is now completed. The fact that an angel blows the trumpet assures the reader that the actions that follow are authorized by God. A long discussion in the Wisdom of Solomon 11–19 is pertinent to this concern. This passage suggests that God sometimes renders condemnation by allowing communities to collapse under the weight of their idolatry, moral failure, and unethical practices. God allows the self-destructive patterns of thought and behavior to destroy the life of the community (e.g., "Therefore those who lived unrighteously, in a life of folly, you tormented through their own abominations" [Wisd. Sol. 12:23]). In addition to direct divine initiatives, then, social circumstances are sometimes themselves agents of judgment.

The hail, fire, and blood of the first trumpet are reminiscent of the similar elements in the seventh plague on the Egyptians (Ex. 9:22–26). They burn a third of the earth, a third of the trees, and all the green grass. Wisdom of Solomon 16:15–24 regards the intermingling of hail and fire (an unexpected combination) as a major demonstration of nature punishing the wicked and idolatrous. In the first trumpet blast, then, elements of nature work against support of life in the world. The chaos in nature as it is now is in marked contrast to the harmony of nature in the New Jerusalem of Revelation 20, where the natural world is in mutually supportive community with humankind.

The second trumpet blast (vv. 8–9) pictures a great burning mountain being thrown into the sea, which turns to blood, as in Exodus 7:20–21. The listener realizes that the mountain is Babylon (Rome) and remembers that in Jeremiah 51:25, God will make of Babylon a burnt earth (cf. Amos 7:4). As noted previously, Mount Vesuvius had erupted in just such a display, leaving the noted city of Pompeii a waste. One of the many associations with fire in the biblical tradition is judgment. According to some of the oldest myths in the ancient Near East, the sea is a source, repository, and symbol of chaos. This part of the vision assures the community that Rome will be returned to the chaos by which Rome has ruled the world. The social chaos of John's world is, in fact, an agency through which God is facilitating the downfall of Rome.

The third blast (vv. 10–11) is not paralleled in the plagues in Egypt. However, when the community hears that a great star falls from heaven, the community will recollect Isaiah 14:1–21, in which the epic prophet Isaiah depicts the downfall of Babylon in similar imagery. The star (Babylon) in the time of Isaiah had claimed for itself the ultimacy and sovereignty that belong only to God. In consequence, Babylon fell. In Isaiah the star is named Day Star or son of Dawn (names of idols). However, John gives the star the name Wormwood, a designation that itself depicts the effects of Babylon (Rome) in the human community, for wormwood was a plant that had a bitter taste. Furthermore, in the First Testament, the disobedient community that has turned to idolatry, injustice, and false prophets, receives wormwood as a part of divine judgment (e.g., Jer. 9:15, 23:15; Amos 5:7, 6:12). The name of the star reveals its effect in the world: It turns the water bitter and it brings judgment. The listener will also contrast the polluted waters of the second trumpet blast (the water turns to blood) and this third trumpet blast (many die from the water because of its bitterness) with the calm sea of the heavenly world (Rev. 4:6), and especially the water in the New Jerusalem, which supports life as God intends it (Rev. 21:6; 22:1–5). The listener will also contrast the falling star of Babylon with the stars (representing the angels that will mediate providence to the churches) that the risen Christ holds in his protecting hand (Rev. 1:20).

The fourth trumpet (v. 12) destroys a third of the sun and other heavenly beings. This blast is similar to the ninth plague in Egypt when the sky turned dark (Ex. 10:21). The ninth plague definitively revealed the superiority of the God of Israel over the deities of Egypt. Both the Egyptians and the Romans had astral deities among their objects of worship. The God of Israel is the sovereign creator of all things whom the elements still obey. This God could turn the sky in Egypt dark, while the Egyptian and Roman deities sit by powerlessly. When the sky turns dark, their secondary status and their impotence are exposed to the whole cosmos. Furthermore, the mention of sun, moon, and stars recollects the story of the creation of the world, in which God began by creating light. On the fourth day, God fashioned the heavenly luminaries. Their existence is a part of the structures that maintain the world as it is. The fourth trumpet blast signals the reader that the structures that have kept the current world in place are now beginning to break down. The fact that the sun, moon, and stars lose only a third of their light indicates that the Roman deities still have some power, and that the deconstruction of the world is not complete. But it is underway.

We can easily summarize the message of this passage and its theological claims. Rome has fallen under divine judgment because of its idolatry, false values, and injustice. God is permitting social conditions within the Roman world, and circumstances in the realm of nature, to function as instruments of judgment. Rome is on its way to collapse. In the larger world of Revelation, we learn that God aims to replace fallen Rome with the New Jerusalem, a world in which all persons, relationships, behaviors, and situations mediate God's purposes. The vision implicitly calls the community to repent of any complicity in these qualities so that they can be gathered into the New Jerusalem.

This claim represents an interesting theological problem. The gospel is the news of God's unconditional love for all and God's will for justice for all. Certainly this text affirms God's desire for the world to manifest these qualities. But while the collapse of Rome ends idolatry, falsehood, and injustice, the collapse causes considerable human suffering and pain in the realm of nature. Some Christians regard this pain as the recompense for the pain that Rome has caused others. However, whether God is the direct agent of judgment, or the one who permits judgment to occur through the internal dissolution that takes place as falsehood corrodes society, these consequences hardly seem consistent with unconditional love and unremitting justice for all. Some Christians believe that while God seeks the transformation of Rome into the New Jerusalem, a loving and just God does not seek for any people or elements of nature to suffer. They reason that while God has more power than any other entity in the world, God does not have unlimited power and hence cannot singularly prevent the march of circumstances toward the collapse of Rome under judgment. God will do all that God can to help lead the world toward becoming a new promised land. In any event, the text itself is a dramatic call to turn away from complicity with idolatry, unfaithfulness, and injustice, as represented by Rome, and to turn toward the one living, true God, and God's ways of love and justice. The text is intelligible in that when we penetrate its imagery, its message is straightforward. It is also consistent with other beliefs and practices of the Christian community. Concerns about moral plausibility are refracted through the concern about appropriateness to the gospel, as noted in step 9 above.

The hermeneutical relationship between the text and today's community falls into the second category that we noted above in step 9, an unintelligible or inappropriate text. The preacher needs to help the community reflect on the questions that arise in connection with questions articulated in the previous paragraph concerning the degree to which the claims of the text are appropriate to the gospel. However, when this question is resolved, then the preacher can use the text as a model by which to help the congregation reflect on the situation of the world today. In the sermon on this text in chapter 4, the preacher finds points at which our culture behaves in idolatrous and unjust ways that are similar to Rome in antiquity. The preacher also names points at which our culture is in danger of collapse.

The preacher hopes that points of similarity between the world of Rome and our world will call the contemporary community to repent. The alternative is to share the fate of Rome. The preacher also hopes to remind us that it is often difficult for us to let go of the known and familiar, and to venture into the unknown and unfamiliar, even when the present is painful and fearful. The preacher assures us that Jesus goes with us into those processes of transformation that involve repentance and letting go of the past, as a part of moving toward a future that is promising but not fully disclosed.

JACOB'S DREAM OF ANGELS
ASCENDING AND DESCENDING: A SAGA

Genesis 28:10–22, the story of a dream in which Jacob sees angels ascending and descending from heaven, is a clearly defined literary unit. The text relates an incident from the life of Jacob. However, the text was given its present form by the Priestly writers about the time of the exile in Babylonia. The Babylonians had overrun Jerusalem, left much of the city depleted, and deported many of the Jewish leaders to a swampy part of Babylon. These leaders found themselves in a land in which the majority population did not speak their language, did not wear their clothing, did not eat their food, and did not recognize the sovereignty of their God, and in which they had to reestablish their ways of achieving economic security and relating to those outside the Jewish realm. Psalm 137 captures the feeling of this historical setting.

> By the rivers of Babylon—there we sat down and there we
>   wept when we remembered Zion.
> On the willows there we hung up our harps.
> For there our captors asked us for songs,
>   and our tormentors asked for mirth, saying,
>   "Sing us one of the songs of Zion!"
> How could we sing the LORD's song in a foreign land?
> If I forget you, O Jerusalem, let my right hand wither!
> Let my tongue cling to the roof of my mouth,
>   if I do not remember you,
>   if I do not set Jerusalem above my highest joy.
>
> (vv. 1–6)

The exile raised profound theological questions for the Jewish community. God made fundamental promises to Abraham and Sarah and their descendents. Why should we continue to count on those promises, asked the community, when our immediate experience seems to deny some of them? The promise of the land was particularly important to Jewish identity. Who are we if we do not possess the land that God gave to us? If God is truly sovereign, why has this exile happened? Can we count on God to keep the divine promises? Is God sufficiently powerful to return us to the land and the life that God promised? What is the point of trying to be faithful to God when we end up in exile?

Genesis 28:10–22 is an etiology. Etiologies are designed to explain the origin of particular places, customs, or beliefs. This passage explains the origin and significance of Bethel, a place that was sacred in Jewish tradition. However, the story has a much deeper meaning. The story is nestled in the wider narrative of Genesis, and in the still wider material shaped by the Priestly theologians that stretches from Genesis through the Chronicles. It is a saga whose purpose is to bespeak the identity of God and of the descendants of Abraham and Sarah. The Priestly writers shaped this story so that it could shape the identity of the exilic community and respond to the questions posed by the exile. These stories reveal the character and power of God, God's continuing relationship with (and promises to) the community, the reason for the exile, and their future as one of hope because it is determined by the sovereign God. God graciously elected Abraham and Sarah to be a means through whom the blessing of God is known among all human families (Gen. 12:1–3). God is always with them and can be counted upon to keep that promise. The exile occurred because of Judah's unfaithfulness. However, God will not abandon this people. Our text partakes of these purposes.

The immediate literary context is the story of Jacob (beginning with Gen. 25:19). The Priestly theologians use the figure of Jacob to represent aspects of the experience of the community. As a descendant of Abraham and Sarah, and Isaac and Rebekah, Jacob is an heir of the gracious promises of God. However, Jacob's character is revealed in the Hebrew meaning of his name: grabber. Jacob, in an act of unfaithfulness, defies custom and wrangles the birthright and the blessing of his parents that should have gone to his older brother Esau. In order to escape Esau's rage, Jacob flees. When we encounter Jacob in our story he is in a position that is reminiscent of the Priestly community. Because of sin, Jacob (and the later community) are uprooted from their homes, in exile, facing an uncertain future. And yet, when Jacob sleeps at Bethel, he receives assurance from God, an assurance that speaks directly to the deepest uncertainties of the people in exile.

The narrative moves from Jacob sleeping and dreaming, through his interpretation of the dream, to the response in which he names the place Bethel, sacralizes it, and makes a vow to offer tithes there. The units of meaning that determine the movement of the sermon are as follows: the setting of the story (vv. 10–11), the dream (vv. 12–15), Jacob's interpretation (vv. 16–17), and Jacob's response (vv. 18–22).

The first item of importance to result from a word by word study of the text is that, initially, the place where Jacob stops is not charged with symbolism. It is simply a place between Beer-sheba and Haran. The dream that occurs gives the place its significance. A traditional interpretation of the stone that Jacob placed around his head is that he used it as a pillow. However, many interpreters today note that a stone would be an uncomfortable headrest, and posit instead that the patriarch laid it alongside his head to serve as protection in case Esau (or a local thief) attempted to thump his head in the night with a club. The stone, then, signals Jacob's anxiety.

People in antiquity often used the motif of a dream to indicate communication between God and the dreamer (vv. 13–15). In the dream, according to the NRSV, Jacob saw a ladder. However, most scholars today think that he saw a ramp. Angels are ascending and descending, indicating that the contents of the dream bring trustworthy news from the heavenly world. God speaks, and confirms that God will eventually return Jacob to the land. Jacob's offspring will be great in number and living west, east, south, and north (i.e., all over the land). And through their subsequent life, the promises to Abraham and Sarah will be fulfilled, for "all the families of the earth shall be blessed in you and in your offspring." God says, further, "Know that I am with you and will keep you wherever you go, and will bring you back to this land." In its biblical contexts, the assertion "I am with you" not only means that God is constantly present, but as is made explicit here, that God is actively working on behalf of those with whom God is present.

When Jacob awakes, he cries out that the Lord is at that place, though he had not recognized it prior to his sleep (vv. 16–17). Because the place previously had no special significance, Jacob had not expected to encounter God there, thus reminding the listeners that they can become aware of the holy in any time and place. Jacob declares that "This is none other than the house of God, and this is the gate of heaven." "The gate of heaven" is an expression that people sometimes used in antiquity to designate places where they received revelation from God. The visual image is of a gate opening between the heavenly and earthly worlds.

Jacob's response (vv. 18–22) is to set up the stone and pour oil on it. In the Mediterranean world, people frequently marked holy places by erecting a monument. The Jewish community used oil to mark things for sacred use. Jacob calls the place Bethel, which means "house of God." Jacob makes a vow that, when God has fulfilled God's promises and returned Jacob to that place, the patriarch will tithe. The tithe was a multifaceted symbol that represented the gratitude of the tither to God, the commitment of the tither to God, and the commitment of the tither to the community and to God's ways of justice for the community. The tithe was one of the means whereby the Jewish community provided for the poor, the widows, the orphans, and others in need. Although Jacob is on the run because he has acted unjustly and has destroyed the fabric of the community of his family of origin, he anticipates the day when his participation in the community will be fully restored.

In sum, God's statement in the dream, reaffirming the promises that God made to the ancestors, is a remarkable demonstration of grace. Jacob has been unfaithful. He has not sought contact with God. God comes to Jacob in the dream at the divine initiative. The patriarch has no claim upon God. Yet God will continue to work through Jacob's life to effect blessing for Jacob and for the other families of the world.

These theological claims are appropriate to the gospel. The emphases on God's promises and grace in this story are certainly consistent with God's unconditional love and will for justice, for Jacob and for those whom he represents. They do not deny God's love or justice to anyone. They are intelligible so that we can understand them, and they are logically consistent with other beliefs and actions that are characteristic of a gospel-shaped community. Some of the motifs of the story are outside of the everyday worldview of most people in the long-established denominations (e.g., a dream as a vehicle of the knowledge of God, and a specific place as the gate of heaven where we see angels). But we recognize these images as drawn from the world of antiquity for which we have contemporary analogies (as developed in the sermon on this passage in chapter 4). The story is morally plausible.

The hermeneutical relationship is the first one mentioned on page 39. Since the claims of the text are appropriate to the gospel, intelligible, and morally plausible, the preacher's call is to encourage the community to name how the text is confirmation, enlargement, or challenge. Given the fact that the sermon below was for a congregation of delegates to an international meeting of a long-established denomination that feels somewhat like it is in exile, the hermeneutical direction of the sermon is confirmation. The sermon seeks to assure the congregation in a way parallel to the way that the dream assures Jacob and the story assures the Priestly community. As previously intimated, the preacher draws analogies between the worlds of the community for whom the Priestly writers shaped this material, and today's congregation. The long-established denomination today finds itself in a situation of exile in North America that is similar to the experience of exile in the days of the Priestly writers. The promises to Jacob (representing the community) are similar to the promises that God speaks to us. God gives us experiences of the divine presence that are akin to Jacob's dream. Just prior to the sermon, we include a flowchart that outlines the sense-units of the text and their relationship to the points of hermeneutical contact with the congregation.

THE SOWER AND THE SOILS
PARABLE AND ALLEGORICAL INTERPRETATION

Mark 4:1–9 is the parable of the sower and the soils, with its allegorical interpretation in verses 13–20. In its Markan context, the two parts of the parable are joined by a short discourse on the meaning of parabolic speech (vv. 10–12). The complete meaningful unit is thus Mark 4:1–20. However, verses 10–12 are difficult to understand both exegetically and theologically. That part of the text requires so much explanation and theological analysis that the preacher did not think it possible to give adequate time in the sermon to both the parable (with the allegorical interpretation) and to the comment in verses 10–12. The preacher would consider these verses in a separate sermon that would allow time to unfold their exegetical meaning and to wrestle with their theological interpretation.

The Gospel of Mark was written shortly after the fall of the temple in Jerusalem in 70 C.E. Aspects of Mark's sociohistorical world are in the background of this story. According to the window into the Markan community that is provided by Mark 13:5–23, the social world of Mark was in disarray. The Markan church, which evidently had a strong Jewish element, was coming into conflict with non-Christian Judaism because of the Gentile mission. Some of the members of the Markan church were being disciplined by the synagogue, even being lashed ("beaten in synagogues"). Some families were coming apart as some family members identified with the emerging Christian movement while others remained in the non-Christian synagogues. Because responsibility to family is central to Jewish identity (represented by the commandment, "Honor your father and mother" [Ex. 20:12]), the separation of parents from children and siblings from each other was extremely serious. Everyday business and social relationships were tense because of the recent war with Rome and the heightened Roman military presence in Palestine in its wake. Some people were dislocated. The community had difficulty distinguishing between true religious leaders and false prophets and false messiahs. The Romans desecrated the temple. The destruction of the temple raised searching theological questions for all in the Jewish orb. Does the destruction of the temple mean that the promises of God are no longer valid? Are we abandoned? What is our future? The parable and its allegorical interpretation suggest that the Markan community was discouraged. Its mission, to preach the gospel to all nations (i.e., Gentiles [Mark 13:10]), seems not to be prospering. Its confidence in God is flagging. This information is crucial to the sermon that appears in chapter 4 on this passage.

These themes are present in the immediate literary context of the parable. After announcing the main theme of his ministry as the manifestation of the rule of God (Mark 1:14–15), Jesus demonstrates the truth of that claim through healing miracles and

exorcisms 1:21–45). He comes into conflict with Jewish authorities who resist the notion that the reign of God is coming to expression through the ministry of Jesus (2:1–3:6). The later listener,
of course, hears an echo of Jewish resistance to the notion that the
church is witnessing to the rule of God. Some Jewish leaders even
accuse Jesus of operating under the power of Satan (Mark
3:19–30). Some of Jesus' relatives (including his mother) seek to
speak with him, but Jesus defines the real community for his followers not as their blood relatives but as "whoever does the will of
God" (Mark 3:31–35). The parable and its interpretation help the
listener make sense of the conflict and confusion that have attended the beginning of Jesus' ministry, and that is a part of their
later common life.

The Gospel of Mark is apocalyptic in its theology. It assumes
that this present sinful age is infested by Satan and the demons,
and is under God's judgment. Through Jesus Christ, God is bringing a new world, often called the reign (kingdom) of God. Jesus'
earthly ministry was the beginning of God's invasion of the world.
According to Mark 13:24–27, Jesus will return to complete the destruction of evil and the installation of the reign of God by means
of a historical cataclysm. According to Mark 13, the author wants
the community to believe that this apocalyptic event will happen
soon. In the meantime, the community needs faithfully to carry out
its mission of preaching to the Gentiles, even in the face of oppo-
sition from outside the community and discouragement within the
community. This theology infuses Mark 4:1–9 and 13–20.

The verse by verse preacher needs to help the congregation understand the literary genre of Mark 4:3–9 and 13–20 because Mark
presupposes a specialized understanding of this material. Mark
4:3–9 is a parable, with 4:13–20 as allegorical interpretation. The
term *parable* was applied to many different kinds of speech in the
world of the first century (e.g., simple comparisons, illustrations,
visions with interpretation, riddles, allegories). The parable in
Mark 4:3–9 is a short narrative; verses 13–20 are an allegorical interpretation that explains the meaning of the different elements of
the parable from the perspective of Mark's situation and apocalyptic orientation. The allegorical interpreter assumes that the various

parts of the narrative have significance that is not obvious to the casual listener but must be brought to the surface. This literary pattern is typical of material identified as parable in apocalyptic literature. The writer provides a narrative or an image that is charged with symbolism. The parable or image proper is then followed by an allegorical interpretation that interprets the meaning of the narrative (e.g., 2 Esdras 4:13–25).

In apocalyptic literature, the purpose of parables, when accompanied by allegorical interpretation, is to disclose some aspect of the coming of the reign of God into the present world. When in company with interpretation, the parables help their hearers discern the "mystery" or "secret" of the rule of God. In this context, the term "mystery" does not mean that which is inscrutable, but is a nearly technical term that refers to the fact that God has hidden the timing and means of the transformation of history from old age to new. Mark uses this parable and its interpretation to help the community discover dimensions of the rule of God and its relationship to their situation of which they may not have been aware.

The story and its explanation fall into easily identifiable units of meaning: setting (vv. 1–2), the sower (v. 3), first seed (v. 4), second seed (vv. 5–6), third seed (v. 7), fourth seed (v. 8), exhortation (v. 9), comment on the disciples' lack of understanding of the parables (v. 13), interpretation of the sower (v. 14), interpretation of the first seed (v. 15), interpretation of the second seed (vv. 16–17), interpretation of the third seed (vv. 18–19), interpretation of the fourth seed (v. 20). In the sermon on this passage in chapter 4, the preacher first discusses the setting of the parable in its immediate literary surroundings and in the historical situation of Mark. In order to help the congregation understand the parable in its Markan frame of reference, the preacher then brings together each element of the parable with its allegorical interpretation. As the flowchart shows at the beginning of that sermon, the preacher discusses the first seed, immediately followed by the allegorical interpretation. The preacher then discusses the second seed, followed immediately by its allegorical interpretation. The preacher follows a similar pattern in connection with the third and fourth seeds.

As pointed out in the word by word study that follows and in the sermon on this text in the next chapter, Mark uses key words and phrases to link the interpretation of the parable with other scenes in the Gospel that probably recall situations in Mark's community. The allegorical interpretation helps interpret those scenes and situations. Those scenes help interpret the parable.

When digging through the text word by word, the preacher first discovers that the setting of the story is designed to create a positive association between the listener and Jesus. Whereas the preceding material has pictured Jesus in conflict with leaders of non-Christian Judaism, the setting portrays a very large crowd around Jesus. They want to hear him. However, Jesus speaks to the crowd only in parables (and does not offer them allegorical interpretation).

The material that follows echoes similar uses of the imagery of seed, sowing, growth, and harvest that is found in apocalyptic literature roughly contemporaneous with the Gospel of Mark (e.g., 2 Esdras 8:26–44; 9:17–22, 29–37; cf. Ecclesiasticus 16:8–9)

The mention of the sower in verse 3 calls to mind a farmer who had prepared the field by working it with a handheld hoe or a basic plow, and then broadcasted the seed. Broadcasting does not allow the farmer precision of aim, so to cover all the space where seed could potentially sprout, the farmer spreads seed everywhere—including on paths, rocky ground, and among thorns. According to the allegorical interpretation, the sower is a preacher who sows the "word." The "word" in Mark is the news of the manifestation of the reign of God through Jesus Christ, to which the church gives witness. The particular calling of the Markan community is to carry this witness into the Gentile world.

The first seed fell "on the path," on the hard soil that has been compacted by people tramping on it day after day (v. 4). Birds could easily eat this seed. In the allegorical interpretation the bird is Satan (v. 15). This phrase "on the path" can also be translated "on the way," an expression that also occurs at Caesarea Philippi in Mark 8:27. Jesus has just revealed that the path to the reign of God takes him through suffering to the cross. Peter protests, so that Jesus responds, "Get behind me, Satan!" Those who deny that suffering is a part of the community's witness to the reign of God are agents of Satan.

The second seed falls on the rocky ground and withers (vv. 5–6). The rocky ground is probably a layer of limestone, common in Palestine, that lies just below the surface of the soil. The allegorical interpretation teaches that these seeds represent people who joyously greet the word but cannot endure the trouble and persecution that come with their witness. Similar language is found in Mark 13:9–13. In the Garden of Gethsemane, the disciples fall away (Mark 14:50). This part of the parable helps explain why some in the Markan church could fall away: They cannot endure.

The third seed falls among thorns that choke it (v. 7). The seed cannot grow in the surrounding vegetation. In the allegorical interpretation this seed represents persons who are choked by the cares of the world (vv. 18–19). These are people who are similar to the rich person who grieves while leaving Jesus because possessions are more important than responding to the reign of God present in Jesus (Mark 10:17–22).

The fourth seed fell into good soil, where it produced thirty, sixty, a hundredfold (v. 8). In Palestine a yield of tenfold was satisfactory; this return is remarkable. The allegorical explanation makes it clear that this imagery is counterpart to similar imagery in apocalyptic texts that represent the fullness of the reign of God (v. 20). The church can count on the coming of the rule of God in the same way that the farmer can count on the seed bearing fruit.

In sum, we note that the parable is a word of encouragement for a congregation that is discouraged with respect both to the results of witness to those outside the community, and to the difficulties that it is facing within. While some people are falling away, the parable calls the church to continue its faithful witness, even through suffering and persecution, because that witness points to the fulfillment of God's hopes for the world that will come into being when the reign of God is manifest. From the extremely modest beginning of the itinerate ministry of Jesus and the preaching of the church (quite a small group compared to the much larger world of Judaism and the massively larger Gentile world), the church's modest efforts at sowing the word are not pointless. They alert people to the almost unimaginable new world that God is bringing.

These claims are appropriate to the gospel in that they assert that God is moving in the world to manifest God's love and God's justice through Jesus Christ and the ministry of the church, and they offer encouragement to a church that seeks to witness to this movement but is growing weary. The claims are also intelligible. We can grasp them easily. They are consistent with other core affirmations and behaviors of the Christian community. They are consistent with our worldview. The theological claims of the passage are also morally plausible in that they do not deny that God loves all and seeks justice for all.

The hermeneutical relationship between the congregation and the text belongs to the first category on page 39. The text assures the congregation that its witness to the gospel is not in vain. Casual onlookers would never have suspected that the reign of God was beginning its invasion of the world through the life, death, and resurrection of the itinerate preacher Jesus. Relatively few believed that the struggling church was an authentic witness to the coming of the cosmic rule of God.

In the sermon on this passage in chapter 4, the preacher uses the message of the parable and its allegorical interpretation to the church in the time of Mark as a model for the gospel message for the church of today. Many leaders and others in the long-established denominations are weary and discouraged. We work hard at sowing, but often the seed does not mature as we expect. The parable assures us that God is present, working through our efforts at sowing, to help manifest the divine rule. Consequently, we can endure.

4

Suggestions for Structuring the Verse by Verse Sermon

All sermons in the form of running commentary share the basic format of exposition of the text section by section. However, within this basic mode, there are many ways to develop the sermon. In this chapter, we describe five possibilities. We illustrate these possibilities with sermons that we have preached in live congregations. Two sermons are from Gil, two are from Ron, and one is from Linda Milavec, an Episcopal priest in Cincinnati, Ohio.

We do not intend our sermons to be models to be emulated. We include them as examples of how three preachers refract running commentary through their own styles and predilections. They illustrate something of the variety that is possible within the mode of running commentary.

The sermons are annotated slightly for two reasons. First, the annotations provide a sense of the occasions when the sermons were preached. Second, the annotations indicate what the preachers were trying to do (and what they hoped would happen in the listening communities).

All five possibilities for structuring the verse by verse sermon share the following ingredients: beginning (introduction), exposition of the text, statement of the contemporary significance of the text, and ending (conclusion). The introduction may be short and simple, or it may be more extensive and developed. The exposition and the contemporary significance may be woven together throughout the sermon, or they may come in large blocks, one following the other.

The preacher may start preparing the sermon with one approach, but in the course of developing the sermon find that another approach is more natural to her or his particular material. A passage may even lead to an entirely different pattern of development, as in sermon E below. Even within a particular pattern, the biblical text may lead to some variation in structure.

Perhaps the most important thing to notice is that some passages are not conducive to sentence by sentence exposition. In most passages, sentences group together in smaller or larger chunks. These chunks are the most natural units of exposition. They may be as short as a word or a figure of speech, or they may be as long as a paragraph. Within a passage, the chunks may even be grouped into larger structures of varied character. The result is that, if the preacher lets the passage suggest the structure, even the options below open into an abundance of variations.

STRUCTURE A. SIMPLE BEGINNING WITH EXPOSITION AND CONTEMPORARY SIGNIFICANCE FLOWING TOGETHER THROUGH THE COURSE OF THE SERMON

The preacher begins with a simple introduction that helps focus the congregation's attention on the passage and that provides information on the historical or literary background of the passage that the congregation needs to understand the passage. The preacher then offers a brief exegesis of a meaningful unit of the passage, followed by a statement of hermeneutical point of contact with that unit. The preacher repeats this pattern throughout the sermon. At the end, the preacher draws the sermon to a close, often by helping the congregation recollect the "big picture" that is communicated by the text as a whole.

Diagram 1 provides a flowchart of how this pattern of preaching moves.

The sermon moves back and forth between the exegesis of the text and hermeneutical points of contact. Often the point of contact is analogical. The preacher helps the congregation envision how our world is similar to the setting, characters, and plot within the text.

Beginning	
Exposition of segment 1	
	Hermeneutical point of contact between segment 1 and the congregation
Exposition of segment 2	
	Hermeneutical point of contact between segment 2 and the congregation
Exposition of segment 3	
	Hermeneutical point of contact between segment 3 and the congregation
Exposition of segment 4	
	Hermeneutical point of contact between segment 4 and the congregation
	Ending

DIAGRAM 1

The first sermon is based on the text that we used as our case study on exegetical method in chapter 3. (see pp. 42–46). The reader can see how one preacher moves from exegesis to the sermon.

"Transfiguration"
Luke 9:28–36
Gilbert L. Bartholomew

The sermon was prepared for a congregation in rural Pennsylvania that, like many congregations, must often deal with difficulties. The preacher takes the story of the transfiguration as a paradigm of how we can face difficulty. After a brief beginning, the preacher interprets the story by moving through the narrative units identified in chapter 3, weaving together explanation and contemporary significance. In connection with each meaningful unit of the text, the preacher offers exegetical interpretation and a hermeneutical point of contact. A brief ending ties together the various pieces of the sermon, making it a meaningful whole.

It does not take much imagination to realize that one of the most common things that threads our lives together is the facing of a challenge. Is there anyone here who is not facing a challenge—anyone who hasn't felt the strain of a broken friendship, a job that leaves you sapped of strength, children who have disappointed you with their choices, unexpected disease, death's all too often premature entry into the lives of our friends and families? Every life I know is touched by the boney fingers of challenge.

Whatever it is, as a Christian you can learn to deal with your challenge *as* a Christian. But doing so means following in the footsteps of one who knew firsthand the downside of dealing decisively with challenges. Jesus began his ministry dealing with common problems of people's daily lives: disease, madness, powerlessness, poverty. He understood his work as part of God's great work of salvation. But as he went along, he discovered that he could not deal with disease, madness, powerlessness, and poverty without stepping on the toes of many people in places of power.

Of course, this happens even in modern America. Just think about how making health care available to all Americans would upset the present system and step on a lot of powerful toes. The challenge to Jesus was at least as big to him as health care reform is to us. And the story of Jesus' transfiguration shows us how he went about facing that challenge. Let's watch what he does as we move through this story.

The beginning of the sermon provides a framework within which listeners can hear the story of the transfiguration. The beginning suggests a common point of contact between their worlds and the world of the text: We often encounter difficult challenges when we try to witness to the gospel in the world. The preacher hopes the congregation will identify with the situation in the text and with the sermon. The preacher directly suggests that the text can help us respond positively to such challenges.

> 28 Now about eight days after these sayings
> Jesus took with him Peter and John and James,
> and went up on the mountain to pray.

When we are about to tackle something challenging, the first thing we often do instinctively is to take a deep breath. Sometimes we do more than take a deep breath. Sometimes we utter a prayer.

Here we see Jesus doing more than taking a deep breath, more than uttering a prayer. We see Jesus getting away for a while in an out-of-the-way place. He takes with him his three closest partners. He gets away for some extended prayer.

Sometimes it is good for us to do that too. We may go to church so we can be with other Christians as we pray about a challenge that lies ahead. Or we may retreat completely from home or work or wherever the challenge lies. We might go alone, or we might go to be with a few people who will share our challenge. More often we simply steal a few quiet moments from dark nights or early dawns, or find solitude in our automobiles.

29 And while he was praying,
the appearance of his face changed,
and his clothes became dazzling white.

30 Suddenly they saw two men, Moses and Elijah,
talking to him.

31 They appeared in glory
and were speaking of his departure,
which he was about to accomplish at Jerusalem.

Sometimes when we face a challenge, especially one we did not choose, instead of taking a deep breath or uttering a brief prayer or going to church or getting away to talk or think things through, we simply try to escape. We want to just run away. Most of the time we cannot do so literally, and so we turn to something that will change our feelings, make us feel good instead of so lousy: alcohol, a buying spree, a video.

Jesus' experience on that Mount of Transfiguration may look at first like such an escape: a paranormal experience during which his body and clothing began to glow and he found himself talking with people who long ago had gone on to glory.

But when we listen to the story closely, we realize that his extraordinary experience was not simply an interlude of good feelings that provided him momentary escape from his challenge. Note that his experience is the experience of a conversation with Moses and Elijah about "his departure, which he was about to accomplish in Jerusalem." The center of his experience was not a brief escape from the challenge, but it was a conversation about the challenge itself. For the "departure" is his death.

Luke says that while Jesus was praying a change came over Jesus' face and his clothing became dazzling white. Was this before, during, or after the appearance of Moses and Elijah? I can imagine that it was the conversation that brought about the change, even though Luke reports it first. As he faced his problem squarely, prayed about it, talked about it with

Moses and Elijah—those reliable guides from the past—he came to experience a deep peace, and it showed, especially in his face. Perhaps lines of worry and fear had appeared on his face before he went up to the mountain as he talked with his disciples about his coming death and the suffering they would have to endure with him if they wanted to be his followers. Now those lines have disappeared and been replaced with a radiant joy, but not the radiant joy that comes from too much alcohol that only masks our problem and leaves us no further along after we sober up than before we began to drink. It is a radiance that comes from having looked our problem straight in the face and been given the gift of a way to face it, a gift that is often as mysterious as the miracle of Jesus' dazzling garments. Ask me to describe why I feel differently, and I may not be able to explain it. I only know I do, and that my new feelings are making it possible for me to face the problem, not run from it.

Let's notice something important about Jesus' experience. As Jesus prayed about his coming journey to Jerusalem and the rejection and death he faced there, the Gospel writer tells us that he was talking with two people—Moses and Elijah. Is it possible that as Jesus prayed, the way he went about praying was to remember the stories of those two leaders of Israel, the Abraham Lincoln and George Washington of his people? One way to pray is to do precisely what the evangelists say Jesus was doing in his vision: carry on a conversation with a character in a Bible story. Luke says that Jesus conversed with Moses and Elijah when they appeared to him "in glory." We will need to converse with the characters of our sacred stories in our imaginations. The word *imagination* often has a negative ring, meaning that something is not real. But imagination can also be a doorway into a very deep reality. Our imaginations are often reliable tools for leading us into the depths of the challenges that lie before us.

Let Jesus be your spiritual guide in learning to pray. Put yourself in Jesus' place for a moment and imagine what he might have said to these two men and what they might have replied. Of course, you need to know their stories and how God worked with them in their own times of trouble. It might be profitable to stay in touch with your own challenge and to read the stories of Moses and Elijah, then to carry on a conversation with them in your imagination about the challenge you are facing.

This important part of Jesus' experience suggests to us two things we might do when we face a great challenge. One is to be sure to talk with someone else about it. It may be someone who has been through something similar before you. I remember that when someone close to me had a rheumatoid disease, she spent some time talking with a good friend because her friend had been dealing with the same thing for a long time. We may find a lot of strength from such conversations: suggestions on how to deal with the problems, assurance that one can face the struggle and still live a significant life, and just the quiet assurance that you are not alone.

We may remember that welcoming Jesus into our conversations is a form of prayer. Jesus promised us that wherever two or three are gathered together in his name, there he is in the midst of us. During our conversation, we need only remember that Emmanuel is with us. Jesus is immediately available as a conversation partner.

Another thing to do is to pick a biblical character who experienced something similar to what you are experiencing, and to carry on an imaginative conversation with him or her. This is also a way of praying. It helps to know your Bible a bit, to have been reading it, so that when something distressing comes along, a character in the Bible comes to mind. But if none does, you can read your Bible to look for such a character. Or you can get on the phone with another Christian, one who knows the Bible a little better than you do, and ask that person to help you find the story of a biblical character to pray with.

> 32 Now Peter and his companions
> were weighed down with sleep;
> but since they had stayed awake,

they saw his glory
and the two men who stood with him.

33 Just as they were leaving him, Peter said to Jesus,
"Master, it is good for us to be here;
let us make three dwellings,
one for you, one for Moses, and one for Elijah"—
not knowing what he said.

Until this point in the story, Luke has been telling us about Jesus' own experience. Here we shift to the experience of the disciples who were with Jesus. We may continue to see things in this story that may help us to meet our challenges as Christians. Before they came up the mountain, they had heard Jesus speak to them of the sacrifice that would be required of them if they wished to join Jesus in meeting his challenging task. The disciples show us how much our feelings can change about a challenge. When we first meet it, we get all worked up with determination or enthusiasm. But it is not long till we get weighed down with weariness, and we are tempted to numb ourselves and to sleepwalk through our times of trouble.

Then something exciting catches us, a glorious vision of the goal of which we dream: a future reconciliation, a miraculous cure, a sudden insight into a seemingly unsolvable problem. And like Peter, we try to sustain that vision and that feeling. In the excitement Peter blurted out something about three tents. It's hard to know what he was talking about, but then Luke says even he didn't know what he was talking about! But he said it as the vision began to disappear—as the ecstatic moments in life all too quickly do. "Why do you have to go so soon, Moses and Elijah? Why not stay for a while? We'll rig up something here to make you comfortable!"

Then suddenly the mood changes again.

34 While he was saying this,
a cloud came and overshadowed them;
and they were terrified as they entered the cloud

The euphoria did not last long. A damp, gray, depressing mist envelops them. The atmosphere has turned from a warm glow to fearful chill. But as they huddled, shivering in the cloud, they heard a clear voice:

> 35 Then from the cloud came a voice that said, "This is my Son, my Chosen; listen to him!"
>
> 36 When the voice had spoken, Jesus was found alone.

Often to us Christians that is all that is left. There is no extraordinary experience, no exciting feelings to carry us through, only the assurance that Jesus is God's Son and the instruction that we are to listen to his word.

> And they kept silent
> and in those days
> told no one any of the things they had seen.

Here is the amazing and curious end to this story. The disciples go into this awesome experience of Jesus in his glory, so soul-shaking that they want to camp there forever, so fearful that they can barely take in what it means. And they say *nothing.* Here is the amazing truth about conflict, about troubles, about challenges, about life itself. We need our wise friends, our counselors, our ancestors in faith, our own inner resources. But when we encounter the very presence of the living God, we are often moved so deeply that we are rendered speechless, left mute in the face of a reality so glorious and so gracious that we had never quite imagined it. We are so close to God's greatness that our words fall away like useless cardboard.

Such moments are wonderful, but even more wonderful is to join a rabbi and his disciples who are now equipped for the rest of their journey. They are now ready to live into the future, buoyed with a faith and energy that will power them for the rest of their lives, whether their days are few or many, no matter what befalls them. And that is true for me and you.

STRUCTURE B. SIMPLE INTRODUCTION WITH EXPOSITION GIVEN IN A BODY FOLLOWED BY CONTEMPORARY SIGNIFICANCE IN A SINGLE BODY AT THE END OF THE SERMON

This sermon begins with a simple introduction that, like the beginning of the previous approach, helps focus the congregation's attention on the passage. The preacher may call attention to an intriguing aspect of the passage, or may suggest a connection between the text and an issue or situation in the setting of the contemporary congregation. The preacher may also provide information on the historical or literary background of the passage that the congregation needs in order to understand it.

The sermon then contains exegesis of the text, segment by segment, but in a single block. The preacher discusses the contemporary significance of the text in a following block of material. The preacher might want to take this approach when the details of exegesis are so closely related that it would be distracting and hard to follow for the preacher to intersperse the exegesis with discussion about the points of contact between the ancient and contemporary worlds.

The ending of the sermon functions much as the ending of the sermon discussed above.

This approach to the sermon is technically a subcategory of the Puritan Plain Style, which consists of introduction, exegesis of the biblical text, application of the text, and conclusion. In the mode of running commentary, the exegesis of the passage always follows the structure of the text itself, whereas the Puritan Plain Style does not require this format. Also, the hermeneutical point of contact in the genre of running commentary may not be an "application." See diagram 2.

"You Don't Have to Impress Me"
Luke 10:38–42
Linda Lee Milavec

This sermon on the story of Mary and Martha moves in the pattern just discussed. It opens with a simple introduction. The preacher identifies

Beginning (seldom more than 10 percent of the sermon)
Exegesis of the text in the form of running commentary (about 40 percent of the sermon)
Statement of the hermeneutical point of contact of the text with the contemporary congregation (about 40 percent of the sermon)
Ending (seldom more than 10 percent of the sermon)

DIAGRAM 2

episodes within the story. She moves with her listeners through the narrative, unfolding the characters and drawing out the scenes. In the exposition, she makes use of narrative implication and brief connections to contemporary culture as she goes. But she saves a contemporary story that suggests the contemporary significance of the biblical story until the end of the sermon.

1. Brief Introduction

Throughout human history people have observed something so frequently that we would be safe in regarding it as a truism: Men and women are *different.*
   • From the first time that pink booties were determined to be wonderful attire for females new to the species,
   • From the moment that young girls were trained in the art of being nice and saw pleasing the other as their very raison d'être,
   • From the dawn of history, as women have given themselves over gladly and joyfully so that their men can be happy and comforted and fed and soothed and loved—people have observed that men and women are different.

However, the question of appreciation and recognition for this kind of total selfless giving has driven a wedge between and expanded the subtle differences between women and men. In today's gospel Jesus stands poised between the sides of this great chasm.

Here the preacher's body mimics her words by standing in the middle of the chancel, placing one leg on each "side" of the story she will be building. Choosing a body posture to carry the structure of the story helps the listeners organize the unfolding story.

2. Luke's Narrative Context

This brief part of the sermon is designed to help the community have a sense of the narrative context in which Luke tells this story. The feelings and intonations of the larger context are presumed within the vignette of Mary and Martha.

As we come into today's story, Jesus, and more than likely his disciples, are on their way—not just any "way," but the way to Jerusalem. That which is heavy and difficult lies before them.

The brush strokes of the story need not always be heavy, even when the words are.

They stop on their way at the house of someone whom Jesus loves, at the house of Martha.

3.   Martha (v. 38)

Now what do we know about Martha? My own impressions are these: I imagine her to be a woman of substance, a woman of some means. We can infer that, like Mary Magdalene, Susanna, and the many other women Luke tells us provided for Jesus and his disciples out of their resources (8:1–3), she supports the rabbi Jesus and his disciples out of her own finances. One of the ways we know her to be a woman of means is by the curious detail of her welcoming Jesus into "her" house. It is curious that it wasn't the house of her father or her brother, Lazarus. Perhaps she was a widow, perhaps single. Either way, it was her house. In addition to being a woman of substance, she seems a bold woman, not bound by conventionality that says a single woman shouldn't be inviting a single man, rabbi or not, into her house anyway! If we are permitted to draw on John's Gospel, the only other Gospel that names Martha, we may add a third characteristic. Remember when Lazarus, Martha and Mary's brother, had died? Everyone is in wrenching pain, sitting around for four days crying their eyes out, saying, "If only Jesus had been here, Lazarus would not have died!" But Martha, Martha is a practical woman. When Jesus charges the stone of her brother's death chamber to be put aside so that the living can come forth, declaring him to be beyond that which their broken dreams had ever suspected, Martha—good old practical Martha—says, "But Lord, he's been in there four days, and he will stink!"

Making reference to other familiar stories within a story not only strengthens the character development, but also harnesses the community's memory of the depth and power of other stories they love but hear rarely.

Now I hope this next image doesn't impugn Martha's memory, but to these three characteristics, I wish to add a fourth. It is a product of her practical nature. I imagine Martha to be not only a bold, practical woman of substance. I imagine her also to be a *pot-banger*. What, you may wonder, is a pot-banger? A pot-banger is a person who bangs pots and pans purposefully in order to draw attention to all the wonderful things she is doing that everyone seems to be ignoring.

4. *Mary and Martha (vv. 39–40)*

Martha is from the Middle East. Abraham and Sarah, who are mentioned in the first reading for today, are her rivals in providing the most outrageous hospitality. She loves Jesus.

She knows he is hot, tired, and hungry. She exudes hospitality. Perhaps she even knows the heaviness of his heart as he approaches Jerusalem. We hear her welcome—with a big gesture—Jesus into her home.

And suddenly [*The preacher moves to the left side of the altar, setting up a quick scene with a few gestures*] we see Martha in the kitchen. She has on her big apron. She has beads of sweat coming from her floured brow. She is stooped over three kinds of soups and one kettle of gourmet couscous, not to mention the bread in the oven. She moves back and forth from the kitchen to the living room [*Here the preacher moves to the other side*], emptying ash trays, filling empty glasses even before they hit the carefully selected color-coordinated coasters. And while she is doing this she notices her sister Mary, sitting there just like she too is "one of the guys," listening to Jesus, talking with him, going back and forth about *life* and *meaning* and *integrity,* even in the face of death. And at first she is OK [*The preacher moves back to the other side*]. But then we hear a murmuring. And a muttering. And more murmuring. And then the pots begin to clatter. And the pans begin to clang. And they bang for the first time not so softly. And then a bit louder. AND LOUDER. AND LOUDER, until everyone in the other room has stopped talking entirely and is looking at one another, saying with their eyes, "What's wrong with Martha?"

Just then, Martha comes out of the kitchen with her hands on her hips [*preacher mimics*] saying [*quietly, forcefully*], "Yo, Jesus. I'm up to my earlobes in work in here. Do you suppose you could tell my sister, Mary, to come and help?"

What's with Martha? Luke leaves us to guess. But usually people bang pots when they are upset. They perhaps feel the need to draw attention to themselves as martyrs or as victims. This fits Martha. She would like to be sitting at Jesus' feet too. But there is so much to do. She is not that brazen to do what is permitted only to men, or to be so selfish as to neglect the needs of her guests! After all, if she does not attend to her guests, who will? Besides, it's her path to being loved, the only path to love she knows. And she wants Jesus to love her.

How many of us know this tension all too well? We need a
reason to be loved, something that makes us special and remarkable. How many times have we asked our loved ones in
subtle and overt ways, "Tell me again, why do you love me?"
Or how many of us have waited year after year for the recognition from another that finally renders us "OK"?

In the meantime, the disciples have been waiting for Jesus
to chase Martha's sister out of the circle. Not only does she
sit with them, but she has the nerve to hog the floor with
her own questions and to think that her views on matters are
worth the attention of everybody, even Jesus! They are de-
lighted when Martha starts banging pots. They detect her
annoyance. It matches their own. And they are glad that if
Jesus is too polite to say anything to Mary about her proper
place, Martha is willing to help him out. But of course Jesus
does not oblige them. "Martha, Martha," he says.

5. What Will Jesus Say?

*This part of the sermon creates dramatic tension within the listener.
How will Jesus respond? Will Jesus' response be adequate?*

At this point in the story [*The preacher steps out of the story
to talk to the audience privately*] every woman who has ever
tried to prepare an entire dinner party by herself, and has ever
spent her entire being on her husband or her children so that
they would thrive and be happy, is now on red alert. What is
Jesus going to say? He'd better get it right. He is on the way
to Jerusalem to be crucified. If he gets it wrong here in this vil-
lage along the way, he may not have to wait till he gets to
Jerusalem! All of the men and women watch for his answer.

*Finding the crux of the problem of a story and building it even higher
by relating it to the cultural/social/political issues of the day is one way
to draw the listeners into the dilemma of text for themselves.*

6. Jesus' Challenge (vv. 41–42)

Jesus is no dummy. One thing he notices is that Martha
does not come out and say, "Yo, Mary, can you give me a

hand?" Better yet, she could have said, "Hey, all of you, come out and help!" She could even have said, "I'm taking a break," and come and joined in the conversation herself. But no. Martha says . . . and this is what Jesus notices . . . Martha says, "Lord, do you not care that my sister has left me to do all the work? Tell her to help me!" Martha is playing the victim. She is setting up one corner of the proverbial triangle. You know how it goes. There is the victim, the bad guy, and the savior. But what's this? Jesus is not interested! This isn't the kind of savior he is. He is not the kind who pits one against another.

"Martha, Martha, you are worried and distracted about many things." He addresses, not Mary, as Martha has asked, but Martha herself.

7. *The Story of Susan (Contemporary Significance)*

This story is the heart of the preacher's effort to help the congregation recognize contemporary significance in the text. The narrative format of this form of appropriation is consistent with the narrative form of the biblical text. Hopefully, hearers will refract Susan's story through their own experience.

The story of Mary and Martha brings to mind a woman I know named Susan. I have known Susan for years. I tell her story with her permission.

Susan spent her entire youth trying to impress a father who could not be impressed. Even being bad didn't get much of a rise from him as he read his newspaper, which seemed to always cover his face after dinner. She married young and, true to form, chose someone just like her father as a husband. But unlike her father, her husband was unemployed and unemployable for years, his ill temper and subtle anger getting in the face of every employer. So Susan took on the financial well-being of her family, working two, and on occasion three, jobs to support them all. By the time her three children were grown they too were something of a disappointment. Nonetheless, Susan set out to finally get her nursing degree so that she might better support her growing family, which now included grandchildren.

Susan was not a confident person. She hated being over-weight. She hated her crooked teeth. She was sure that no one could ever find her interesting enough to talk to. Her first week on the job as a nurse she lifted a patient much too heavy and wrenched her back so badly that for the next two years she could barely walk. But because it was her first week on the job she was too afraid to file for workers' compensation, fearing her new employers would simply see her as a slacker. So she continued working full-time, afraid of what would happen to her family if she quit.

One day after work Susan was doing the weekly grocery shopping, dragging her painful leg behind her. She had coupons in her hand and was looking for sale items for which she could use her coupons, thinking that she could double the value of her coupons this way. As she walked down the aisles she was thinking, "Aren't you proud of me, God? Aren't you proud of me? I'm going to save this money for my family, and some for the church too. Aren't you proud of me?" Then she suddenly stopped short. The hair went up on her arm. She heard a voice, a voice quiet and stern within her, say, "You don't need to impress me Susan! You don't need to impress me."

8. Jesus' Gift (vv. 41–42)

As noted earlier, the ending of the sermon comes in a few, quick sugges-tive sentences. This ending offers the congregation a vivid point of con-tact between the sermon and their own worlds without belaboring the point.

What a gift Jesus gives! When Mary, Martha's sister, sat at his feet, she was learning, deeply learning about a different kind of Father that Jesus himself loved to the core of his be-ing, to the tip of his sandals. This is the kind of God who doesn't need us to impress him. This God does not need any of our roles, or projects, or accomplishments tattooed like resumes onto our souls to get his attention. This is the kind of God who doesn't mind the dust bunnies of our sorrows, covered up to impress the big guest. This God, this Jesus, presents himself [*gesture toward the altar*] as a simple meal, an unpretentious gift, a quiet change. This is the kind of Abba who doesn't need us to wear our many necessary activities and roles as if they were long black coats worn in the height of summer, who doesn't even remember our many failures. This rabbi loves us for ourselves. Yes, caring for others can be a fruit of God's gracious love. But it is not what makes us lovable to him. Before we can love our neighbor well, we need to be freed to love ourselves—not our role-playing selves, not our recognition-craving selves, not our irritated, pot-banging selves, but our unaccomplished, God-created selves. Jesus welcomes us to come and sit with him. We may pour out our questions, share the insights that excite us, or just sit quietly in his presence. Jesus invites us to let other things go no matter how pressing they feel. He invites us to love ourselves well enough to sit with him while the pot-bangers loudly pound out their irritation. He invites us to let him love us for ourselves, without regard for anything we can do.

STRUCTURE C. EXTENDED INTRODUCTION (DEVELOPING HISTORICAL, LITERARY, OR THEOLOGICAL CONSIDERATIONS IN SOME DETAIL) FOLLOWED BY EXPOSITION AND CONTEMPORARY SIGNIFICANCE FLOWING TOGETHER

Some biblical passages require more background than can be provided in a simple, short introduction to the sermon. A text may presume cultural or historical background that is unfamiliar to modern readers but that is important for understanding the passage. The writer may make use of a literary style or technique that has particular purposes that are not well known to the contemporary community. A pericope may deal with a problem that is easily misunderstood because of differences in ancient and contemporary contexts. A text may raise a theological or moral issue that needs to be carefully framed in order for the congregation to hear the contribution of the text to the interpretation of that issue. The preacher can provide the necessary background in an extended introduction that develops historical, literary, or theological considerations in some detail. The sermon then moves in the same way as structure A (above).

"Cultural Terminal Illness?"
Revelation 8:6–13
Gilbert L. Bartholomew

The sermon that follows moves in this way. The text is the beginning of the vision of the blowing of the seven trumpets. As in the preceding vision in Revelation 6:1–8—the breaking of the first four seals of the horses of the apocalypse—the blowing of the first four trumpets is a clear grouping within the larger series of seven trumpets. All four release disasters in nature. All four are quite short. The fifth and sixth trumpets are elaborate images of armies of bizarre creatures visiting torture and death on human beings. The first four are also separated from the succeeding trumpets by the appearance of an eagle crying, "Woe, woe, woe!"

The exposition deals with the primary details of the first four trumpets. The preacher decided to treat the elements of the text slightly out of sequence because of patterns of literary relationship within the text itself and within the larger world of the Bible. The first two details, the mountain hurled into the sea and the falling star, come from the beginning of the second and third trumpets. They form a pair—the first having been used by Jeremiah, the second by Isaiah—as symbols for mortal Babylon. John saw Babylon embodied again in the terminally ill Rome of his day. Succeeding generations of interpreters have seen their own tottering civilizations in these symbols. The rest of the exposition takes up the destruction of a third of the trees, sea creatures, rivers, fountains of water, and heavenly bodies. The preacher follows these details in succession, and relates them to the ominous environmental disasters of the twentieth century.

Gilbert Bartholomew's method of interpreting this difficult text is to begin with the meaning of the images within the political and literary world of the first century. He then seeks parallels between the world of the text and the contemporary world. The parallels are to situations in which aspects of life are collapsing. The preacher identifies parallels to phenomena for which preacher and listeners bear some responsibility. The preacher does not project the contemporary problems suggested by the ancient images on forces that are altogether external to the pastor and the congregation. That would too easily give the congregation an escape from taking responsibility for their thoughts, feelings, and actions. The theological underpinning that the preacher commends is rooted in Jesus' summons to trust God to give us a new dimension of life if we are willing to let go of life as it is and to be responsible stewards of God's world while we dwell in it.

The exposition and contemporary significance flow together in the body of the sermon. Toward the end of the message, the preacher steps back to ask, How might we as Christians respond to a terminal diagnosis of our civilization?

Forrest was a big, strapping man, fifty-one years of age. He drove a cement truck and worked hard six days a week. He played hard on the seventh day, hunting in the mountains or working on engines in his shop out back. He ate great slabs of well-marbled steak with mounds of mashed potatoes, but had never had a sick day in his life. He didn't drink, but he smoked a pack a day.

One day driving home from work it hit him—pain like he'd never known since his brother stabbed him in the arm with a hunting knife at age fourteen. Except this time it was in his chest. He pulled over to the side of the busy road, and then everything went blank. He woke up flat on his back all wired up on a hospital bed. The doctor told him he had suffered a severe heart attack and needed bypass surgery or he would die. During the next four days Forrest had plenty of time to think. He thought about bypass surgery. He thought about death. He had never thought about death before, at least not his own death. He knew his chances were good for pulling through. But there were always a few who never woke up. Would he be one of them? Death had never before been such a real possibility for him. He began to think about how he would try to live life differently if he was given another chance. Would he stop abusing his body? Would he spend more time with his wife and teenage daughters?

Would he even begin to go to church, as his wife had been begging him for years? He hadn't thought much about God, but maybe it was time. He picked up a Bible from the table next to his bed. He opened it, wondering. Did it perhaps have a word for him?

The book of Revelation may very well be compared to a doctor's diagnosis, not about individual human beings but rather about human civilization. As a diagnosis about our civilization, it is confirmed by many second opinions by the doctors of our day who are looking at how life is shaping up in our world.

The beginning of this sermon draws a parallel between the diagnosis of a terminal illness of an individual person and Revelation's diagnosis of the terminal illness of a civilization. It suggests that John's vision of the mortal disease of Roman civilization may be uncomfortably true of twentieth-century civilization.

It wasn't too long ago that people were feeling a sense of power about life, a great optimism about the future and particularly about what human beings would be able to do. In the 1960s there were incredible things written about what the future would hold because of human power, particularly human technology and science. We saw a bigger and bigger pie in terms of the resources of the world. We talked about making life artificially, and we still are. We talked about curing all diseases. We even talked about being in the awkward position of having to manage death. We would finally conquer it. Yet it was unreasonable to think that we could stand to have everybody who was born live forever, and so we would have to manage death by finding an acceptable way of getting rid of people.

Theologians were beginning to say that God had to have a new job description. We had eliminated the traditional things that God was supposed to have done, namely, manage life. And if we were going to continue to believe in God, we were going to have to find something else for God to do, something other than simply fill in the gaps where the things were that we weren't able to do ourselves.

But it wasn't long till we began to hear the scientists say that, in the midst of all this wonderful progress, we had in fact been neglecting the world that we had been depending on. We had been abusing it and playing around with dangerous things, so dangerous that some think it is even a miracle that we have survived so far. Certainly it will be a miracle if our civilization makes it to the end of the century. This was John's diagnosis for Roman civilization about two thousand years ago, and since John's time people at various points in history have heard in it the Word of God for their own civilization. Particularly when things got rough, as during years of the great plagues in Europe, people saw in John's visions and began to hear in his words the Word of God for their time. The test here is to see if John's visions are an adequate vision for our time, given what we see going on around us, and if John's visions do in fact contain a Word of God for us. Let us examine this text together.

In this passage from Revelation, two details are particularly interesting. One is the burning mountain being cast into the sea. The other is a falling star, which pollutes the waters of the world. Some interpreters have considered these to be primitive descriptions of cosmic phenomena— comets, for example, or meteors landing on the earth. Others have seen in them cryptic descriptions of nuclear missiles.

The preacher helps the congregation name other ways of interpreting this part of the book of Revelation that the congregation may have encountered on the radio or television, in print, or in Bible study groups. The preacher implicitly invites the community to evaluate these ways of thinking in light of the historical and literary critical approach taken in the sermon.

In fact, these two images were originally symbolic ways of talking about Babylon, the great Babylon, that conquered Israel about six hundred years before Jesus. Babylon was the superpower of the day, and it aspired to be God. Jeremiah and Isaiah both condemned Babylon using these very images of a burning mountain cast into the sea and a falling star that had attempted to ascend to heaven and be above the stars created by God.

John, the author of the book of Revelation, identified Rome as the Babylon of his day, and so he spoke about Rome in the same terms that Jeremiah and Isaiah spoke of Babylon. As we listen to the Bible we begin to wonder whether the same things that are said by visionaries like John about his own time are perhaps true also of our time, or becoming true.

Certainly the picture from this passage of Revelation of extensive destruction is appropriate for our time. I am not saying that these are *predictions* that today this is what John had in mind, but they are *fitting* for our time. Take, for example, the destruction of a third of the trees. A third of the trees are destroyed in our time, not by fire but by acid rain. An article in a magazine I read just the other week said that a third of the forests in Germany are dying because of pollution in the air.

Or consider the image of a third of the living creatures in the sea dying, in our case not because of blood, but because of chemical waste. I spent some time on the island of Crete in the Mediterranean, a sea that used to be teeming with life. I went swimming off the coast with a face mask on. And there wasn't a fish to be seen. There are still fish in the Mediterranean, because the fishermen go out and they make a catch. But it certainly has been greatly reduced from what it was at one time, and because of human neglect and abuse.

The rivers and fountains—we don't poison them with wormwood but by chemical waste seeping down through the soil from our dumps or dumped directly into the rivers. Someone said a little while ago that Long Island had about ten years before it would have to start importing water because all of its groundwater would be polluted. I don't know if that is turning out to be true or not, but it certainly was a threat.

In the vision that a third of the light in the sun, the moon, and the stars would be blotted out perhaps one can even see something of what happens with air pollution today. I was talking with a neighbor several years ago while we stood on the hill that we live on looking out to Hawk Mountain. As we gazed at the mountain through thick haze, he said, "You know, I remember when I was a kid, you rarely saw a day like this. It was a lot more brilliant and clear."

So certainly these images we see in John's visions are appropriate for the things we see going on around us. We would do well to ask the question, Is there a word of God here for us? Perhaps God is speaking to us, much as God spoke to Israel in the days of Isaiah, and much as God spoke to the early Christians in the days of John:

> Though you have called upon my name,
> you have strayed far from me.
> You worship the things you have made.
> You look to them for your security.
> You indulge in them for your own pleasure,
> neglecting and abusing creation,
> neglecting and abusing your brothers and sisters.
> You are like the wicked servant
> put in charge of the others to see to their welfare;
> but you think that because I have not yet come
> I will not come for a long time
> and you can get drunk and knock your brothers and
>   sisters around.
> Till now, like a good mother or father, I have rescued
>   you from
> many of the consequences of your behavior.
> But sadly, it seems
> that the only way to wake you up to what you are
>   doing
> is to let you reap some of the fruits of what you are
>   doing.

Every human being is mortal. But so is civilization. Many civilizations have risen and fallen. For us to think that the same thing can't happen to ours is sheer folly.

The preacher has now finished the exegesis of the text, and identifies several ways that the congregation can respond to the central thrust of the text and its implication for the contemporary setting. He helps the community name these possibilities so that they can critically evaluate them and make a conscious choice to respond in a way that is appropriate to Christian witness.

So when we hear people talking about our world in the way John talks about it in this vision, we have a number of possible responses.

One of the first responses people make to an announcement that death is on its way is denial. God will protect us, or we will save ourselves. We don't really need to change. We can just rely on someone or something coming to the rescue. If we are going to think that, we had better ask ourselves, "Are we better than Israel?" After a long time of grief over what Israel was doing, recorded especially by a prophet like Jeremiah, God finally said that the only way is to let Israel go.

Or we might respond by saying, "Well, the end is coming. Eat, drink, be merry, for tomorrow we die. Might as well be us who use it up." There are people who are saying this about our world.

Or we might respond like people in a theater that's on fire, trampling everybody else down in a mad rush to save ourselves.

There is another alternative. In the face of the real possibility of the disappearance of those things we hold dear, we can stand in awe and appreciation, seeking a new sense of how great the gifts are that surround us, which we have overlooked or taken for granted. Isn't this why God gives us the days we have on earth? We will not live forever, even if our civilization will.

So what is the point of living? Is it not to be confronted with the mystery of life, with its beauty and the abundance of God's gifts, even in the midst of some of the most terrible things?

Revelation 8:6–13 does not directly contain a statement of good news. The preacher must turn to the larger theological framework of the book of Revelation and to the Christian doctrine of providence in order to identify the good news for this sermon. The calamities described by text and preacher can prompt the community to repent and to turn to God and God's ways.

We spend an awful lot of time devoting ourselves to securing our future, both our personal future and our national future. Is it not in the end an exercise in futility? Does life not have another purpose about which the Bible tells us? Are we not to listen more closely to the words of Jesus:

> Don't be anxious about tomorrow.
> Seek first the kingdom of God.
> And God will provide what you need for the morrow in order to live.

At the moment we are faced with the mass destruction of one thing after another in our environment. We are feeling the effects of it. These are warnings to us of the need to repent.

But it is useful also to take seriously the possibility that John holds out in the rest of the book of Revelation: Repentance. Repentence will not be forthcoming from most of the people of the earth, and our civilization is not merely threatened, but is terminally ill with the things that are going on around us.

If indeed our civilization is terminally ill, if as some say we have maybe ten years, what do we want to do with the gifts of time and strength and creativity and physical resources with which we have been endowed? If security is not a realistic goal to pursue, what is the worth of all these things? What is it that God wishes us to do with these gifts, this abundance of gifts that he has given us?

By ending the sermon with a question, the preacher hopes to prompt the congregation to continue thinking about how they can be faithful witnesses with the resources God has given them. The preacher stops talking, but the congregation's participation in the sermon continues as they

*ruminate on the preacher's question from the perspective of their own re-
sources and opportunities.*

> Let us pray.
> Master of the universe,
> You have created the world a good and beautiful gar-
>   den
> and set us in the midst of it
> to tend it and to enjoy it and to share it.
> We have neglected and abused it,
> to the sorrow and agony of ourselves and of our
>   brothers and sisters
> the world over.
> We thank you for this gift,
> and for the abundance of your mercies still available
>   to us
> in spite of our poor stewardship.
> Most of all we thank you for the message of your
>   forgiveness
> and for your promise to create the world anew,
> for your call to repentance
> and for the power of your Holy Spirit to begin to live
>   new lives.
> Teach us to live each day as though it were the
>   special gift it actually is.
> Draw us away from anxiety about the future
> and from frantic efforts to save our own life.
> Instill in us a reverence for life,
> and a desire to care for the neglected and wilting
>   flowers around us,
> and a childlike trust that if we give all we have to this
>   day
> you will supply our need in the days to come,
> and at last raise us up to new life in the eternal
>   kingdom
> which you have prepared for us
> when the travail of creation is at an end
> and you bring heaven and earth to new birth. Amen.

STRUCTURE D. EXTENDED INTRODUCTION WITH EXPOSITION GIVEN IN A SINGLE BODY FOLLOWED BY CONTEMPORARY SIGNIFICANCE IN A SINGLE BODY AT THE END OF THE SERMON

In structure D, as in structure C, above, the preacher needs to provide extensive historical, literary, or theological background. However, as in structure B, the preacher discusses the text, as a whole, in one part of the sermon, and the contemporary significance (again, as a whole) in another part of the sermon.

We see this approach in the following sermon on the story of Jacob's ladder. The extended beginning to the sermon recounts, with the help of current analogies, the events in the story of Jacob that lead to this episode. After this lengthy beginning, the preacher retells the episode itself, interspersing exegetical comments that are designed to help the congregation enter the world of the story. The preacher delays a comprehensive statement on the importance of the story for the congregation until the end of the sermon.

"The Gate of Heaven"
Genesis 28:10–22
Ronald Allen

The following sermon was preached in a local congregation in St. Louis, Missouri, on a Sunday morning when the General Assembly of the preacher's denomination, the Christian Church (Disciples of Christ) was meeting in the same city. About half of the worshiping congregation were, like the preacher, attending the Assembly. The introductory part of the sermon places the passage in its context in the ancestral stories. The middle part of the sermon is running commentary. The final part of the sermon embodies the main learning from the text through a short series of images.

As our story begins from the Bible, Jacob has something in common with many of us: He is on the road. His new lightweight suitcases are about to pop. Jacob sees a gas price along the interstate. "Not bad. Maybe I ought to stop. But, no, the gas prices may be cheaper at the next interchange."

His low-fuel light then comes on, and he pulls into a mini-mart. And wouldn't you know, gas is ten cents a gallon higher than any other place on the whole trip.

As he reaches for his wallet, I imagine he feels a kind of emptiness around his heart. Jacob is leaving home—for a long time. Jacob is not on his way to a General Assembly. He is on the run.

Jacob has a twin, Esau. While the twins were still in the womb, they wrestled and fought. When it came time to be born, Esau started down the birth canal first—but Jacob grabbed him by the heel. You see, the birthright belonged to the firstborn. The birthright was a double share of the inheritance. Jacob wanted a piece of that double share.

In Hebrew, the name *Jacob* means "grabber." And Jacob turned out to be just that—a grabber. Many years later, Jacob and Esau are young men. Esau is a hunter. He lives for meat. But one day he comes home from the hunt empty-handed. He is hungry. Can you feel his stomach constricted, tight, famished? Jacob is making a pot of lentil soup. Can you see Esau, standing beside the fire, belly tight, weak? Jacob looks up from the smoke and he says, "I'll trade you the birthright for a bowl of this fresh, hot soup." And the birthright is gone.

Esau still has one more thing that Jacob wants—the blessing. It too belongs to the oldest child. When the father is old and nearly blind, he is ready to pass the blessing to the oldest son. So Jacob wraps himself in animal skins and, disguised as his hairy brother, goes into his father's dim tent. The old man calls out, "Is that you, Esau? Have you come for the blessing?" Jacob replies, "Yes." The old parent lays hands upon Jacob and the blessing is his. It cannot be taken back.

Esau is enraged. He has made his living by killing. He knows what to do and how to do it. They did not have seminars in conflict management in those days, so Jacob does the only thing he knows how to do. He runs. As I picture it, he has to leave town so fast that he does not have time to stop by AAA and pick up a map.

The sermon moves to the pericope for exposition. I try to help the congregation identify with Jacob. I explain Jacob's situation and then offer four brief analogies from the worlds of the congregation.

Now night is falling. Jacob is in the middle of nowhere and there's not a motel in sight. One night last fall I was driving home from rural Indiana about 11:00 P.M. when my car quit. Nothing to do but get out and walk. So quiet you could hear the heartbeat of the crickets. Rustle. Rustle. Rustle. "What was that?" Snap! "Don't shoot. I don't have enough insurance for my wife and children." It is frightening to be on the road alone at night. In those days travelers planned carefully where they could stop so that they would not be alone in the night, alone in the stormy weather, alone in the face of the wild animals, alone in the dark with thieves. But Jacob is in such a hurry that he has not planned well. The night gathers like a shroud around him. Can you feel with him—alone, on the road, tired, but sensing the need always to look over his shoulder?

Sometimes we are similar to Jacob. We grab. And we find ourselves on the road, at night, afraid. A child in a grocery store slips a piece of candy out of one of those big, clear, glass, wide-mouth jars. All the way out of the store, the child is nervous, looking around. The child can hear the dull clank of the closing of the door of the cell.

When we were in Zambia a couple of summers ago, we saw people thirty-five, maybe forty, years old who looked twice that age. Toothless. Faces wrinkled. Bodies emaciated. "They must live in a drought area?" No, no drought in Zambia right now. "How did they get that way?" They live in an area where they grow sugar. They used to have their own gardens where they grew a balanced diet on a barter economy. But westernization brought a cash economy. They use all of their land for sugar now. And they never make enough money to buy the kind of food they used to grow. So this is what happens to them. Human bodies wasting, so that you and I can grab a bowl of Frosted Flakes for breakfast.

Sometimes we are like Jacob in the church too. Students

graduate from seminary, full of enthusiasm and idealism. You see them at a pastor's conference in a few years, and inevitably someone says, "My love for Christ and my desire to serve him are still very high. But the politics . . . in the congregation, in the region . . . I've sold myself a hundred times already."

Now the sermon interprets the details of the story. Occasionally, I offer an illustration or analogy to help clarify a point or to help the congregation identify with a character, thought, or action.

So night falls, and Jacob finds a place to sleep. He gets a stone. Is it for a pillow? Have you ever used a stone for a pillow? Many interpreters think that Jacob gets the stone not for a pillow but for protection.

Jacob sleeps. I imagine it as a fitful, tossing sleep. And in his sleep, he sees his vision. We usually think of it as a ladder, but the Hebrew language makes it clear that it was more like a ramp, similar to one of those big earth ramps that construction companies build when they are making a superhighway, or similar to a handicapped-accessible ramp. Think of that: heaven as handicapped-accessible. Angels are coming down and going up. And at the top of the ramp—the shining of the glory of God.

Why this ramp? Why to Jacob? Why to the grabber, of all people? How can Jacob possibly deserve this?

But when you take a step back from the story, you see that that is exactly the point. Jacob does not deserve it. By all rights, Jacob ought to be sentenced to pastor's class or confirmation class for life. But God has made promises to Jacob.

God has promised Jacob land, a place of his own. Somewhere in this universe I'll bet there's a little corner where you go when you need to splice your wires and reconnect. God has promised that to Jacob.

God has promised Jacob offspring. In that world, children were three things. First, a sense of future, a sense of the significance of your life that would go beyond yourself. Second, social security in your old age. They furnished your food, clothing, housing. Third, a community. Children were with you day by day. And they stood between you and dying alone.

God has promised to be with Jacob, rejoicing in all of Jacob's joys, feeling every one of Jacob's pains, walking with Jacob every day, every moment, every breath. God has promised these things to Jacob in all of Jacob's Jacobness. No preconditions. No sitting nervously outside some loan officer's office to see if his credit is approved. God made these promises to Jacob's grandfather and grandmother, Abraham and Sarah. God made these promises before Abraham was circumcised, even before Abraham and Sarah had faith. God's promise is God's promise. And it is backed up by the integrity of the divine being.

I can feel Jacob under the night sky, his life flashing before him, the rock near his head, feeling the electricity of the divine presence. Can you?

Jacob cries out, "Surely this is none other than the house of God, the gate of heaven." The gate of heaven is a place where the angels come down and God's promises and presence come into view. The dream is a sign of God's promises for Jacob, a reminder that God is constantly with Jacob.

The exposition has come to the major conclusion in the preceding paragraph. I now offer three images designed to help the congregation reflect on how they encounter the gate of heaven opening in their own worlds.

This affirmation can help us in direct ways. For instance, we are an aging denomination. Our average age more than qualifies us for AARP discounts. But young people do encounter God among us. Take Easter morning when the pastor's class is baptized. You can see their faces shining when they come up out of the water, and you know the gate of heaven has opened.

Or you have one of *those* weeks. You come into the sanctuary on Sunday morning feeling like a burned-out house. Communicating with your children by means of threats. Haven't had time to clean house. Haven't had a complete sentence from your spouse for a week. At the office, the increase in your share of your health insurance is greater than your raise, so that you actually bring home less money than you did last year. And as you are leaving for worship, your dog growls at you.

The service clanks along. You get to the Lord's Table. The elders fumble through their prayers and the deacons can't quite remember where to move or when. But you take the bread and the cup in your hands, and you feel a sense of fullness well up inside of you. It's as though the gate of heaven opens, and the angels come down.

A few weeks ago, I was in a congregation on Sunday morning. A person stood to play the violin—a couple of classical pieces that made your heart throb with surging energy, passion, fire. Then the violinist played, "God's Eye Is on the Sparrow." I look around and half the congregation was weeping. I thought, "This is grade C music." I didn't understand why the congregation was crying.

After the service, someone told me that six months earlier the violinist was in prison. When he got out, he was homeless. Our downtown congregation, which at that time had barely enough members to have the Lord's Supper on Sunday morning, found him, helped him find a job, became his friends, and got him a violin. It is not grade C music when he plays, "God's Eye Is on the Sparrow."

About two years ago, a friend with whom I had gone to school, a minister in another denomination who lived six hundred miles away, called late at night with tragic news—AIDS. As the illness moved through its final stages, he had the night sweats. Cancer sores covered his body. One piece of his life after another had fallen away. He had heard hardly a word from his denomination.

But a Disciples couple had him—a minister under fire in his own congregation—in their home. They drove my friend back and forth to the doctor. They sat with him through the night. They held him.

Even as he was wasting away, he seemed to keep his wry sense of humor. On the phone, I asked him, "How can you be funny at a time like this?" And he replied, "I'm not doing this by myself. I'm not alone."

I heard it. Didn't you? I heard the gate of heaven open. It

opened for Jacob. For my friend. And God promises that it opens for you.

STRUCTURE E. INTRODUCTION WITH EXPOSITION OF PAIRED ELEMENTS IN A TWO-PART PASSAGE, TAKEN UP A PAIR AT A TIME

Some texts, especially allegories, consist of two parts that are closely related. Indeed, the elements within these texts are paired; one element in the first part of the text corresponds to an element in the second part. The preacher can sometimes help simplify the sermon and keep the lines of interpretation clear by discussing the elements of the pair at the same time.

Mark 4:1–9 is the parable of the sower. Mark 4:13–20 is the allegorical interpretation of the elements of the parable. The preacher's task is to help the congregation understand the parable and the allegorical interpretation in both their historical and contemporary dimensions.

Both the parable and the allegorical interpretation consist of four corresponding parts. In addition, as in a typical joke, the first three parts of both the parable and the allegorical interpretation form a set of negative incidents, while the fourth part introduces a surprising positive contrast. Mark assumes that the listeners will hear the story from the perspective of their situations and of Mark's address to their situations as Mark develops it in the Gospel. We are to hear the parable with these concerns in our ears.

The preacher begins the sermon by setting the metaphor of a farmer sowing seed in the cultural and scriptural context of first-century Palestine. Then the preacher takes up the first three negative parts of the parable one at a time. He expounds on each of these parts with the help of the corresponding allegorical interpretation, then on other passages in the Gospel of Mark in which this interpretation comes home to roost, and finally by commenting on the significance of each part for contemporary life. The preacher uses motifs of contrast in the fourth part of the sermon. He moves directly from the parable to a long story that develops the positive implication of the fourth element of the parable.

This pattern is represented by diagram 3.

Beginning: the setting of the story in Mark 4:3 and its interpretation in Mark 4:14		
Exegesis of the pair of elements in Mark 4:4 and 4:15		
	Connection with other material in Mark	
		Hermeneutical point of contact
Exegesis of the pair of elements in Mark 4:5–6 and 4:16–17		
	Connection with other material in Mark	
		Hermeneutical point of contact
Exegesis of the pair of elements in Mark 4:7 and 4:18–19		
	Connection with other material in Mark	
		Hermeneutical point of contact
Exegesis of the pair of elements in Mark 4:8–9 and 4:20		
		Hermeneutical summary of the main teaching of the sermon with the help of a story from Dan Wakefield

DIAGRAM 3

"When the Soil Is Hard"
Mark 4:1–20
Ronald Allen

This sermon was prepared for a conference of clergy in one of the long-established denominations. Many clergy in congregations in these denominations are discouraged and beaten down. The text was chosen and the sermon developed with the hope of encouraging such pastors. The text is divided into three parts: (1) the parable proper in 4:1–9, (2) an explanation of the reason for speaking in parables in 4:10–13, and (3) the allegorical interpretation of the parable in 4:14–20. I decided that the interpretation of the parable would require so much attention that it deserves its own sermon. Hence, I do not treat that part of the text in this message. Furthermore, I interpret the parable proper in the light of its allegorical interpretation in order to give an exposition of the parable proper as it is understood in the Gospel of Mark. As a part of the latter process, I draw connections between this pericope and other pericopes in the Gospel of Mark. In order to use the sermon to concentrate on the parable itself, I discussed the setting (Mark 4:1–2) in the introduction to the reading from the Bible. At the same time, I mentioned why I would not treat verses 10–13. I also invited the congregation to keep their Bibles open. This sermon illustrates a way by which the preacher may ask a congregation to refer to the printed text during the sermon.

"A sower went out to sow" (Mark 4:3). Can you picture it in your mind? A peasant in a rough woven shirt. A bag of seed wrapped around the waist. Taking a handful of seed from the bag and with a practiced movement broadcasting it over the field. Seed. Planting. Fertility. Generativity. It echoes Genesis 1. The broadcasting of the seed calls to mind the force of life and moves through creation itself.

In the world of the first century, the mention of seed and harvest would call to mind something more. The Jewish people often used the actions of sowing and harvesting to speak of the religious life. We can see an example of this use if we turn to Sirach, a book in the Apocrypha written just before Mark. Let us look at Sirach 6:19.

[Pause while people turn to the passage.]

"Come to [wisdom] like one who plows and sows, and wait for her good harvest." Another book written about the time of Mark, 2 Esdras, says more. The passage is chapter 8, verse 41.

[Pause while people turn to the passage.]

"For just as the farmer sows many seeds in the ground and plants a multitude of seedlings, and yet not all that have been sown will come up in due season, and not all that were planted will take root; so also those who have been sown in the world will not all be saved."

Sure enough, in the interpretation of the story, Mark makes just this kind of move. We go now to the allegorical interpretation of the story beginning at verse 14.

[Pause while people turn to the passage.]

"The sower sows the word." Mark has already told us the meaning of "the word." "The word" is the news that the time is fulfilled and the rule of God is at hand (Mark 1:14–15). God is breaking into this old age of brokenness, alienation, and violence—the world of ethnic cleansing and tribal warfare and social violence. And God is coming with a new world of community, justice, peace, and life. God is coming in Jesus of Nazareth. In his life, on the cross, and in the resurrection.

I try now to help the congregation—composed mainly of preachers—to identify with the text.

The sower sows the word. That is what we try to do on Sunday morning. You try to get the best seed that you can. Maybe it has fallen down between the cracks of the pages of the Bible and you have to scrape it out. Or you try to catch it out of the air as it blows by when you are listening to the news. Or you try to hold onto it when it gets passed to you from the clammy hand of a parishioner dying of cancer. You put it down on a few scraps of paper, you practice to the empty pews, and on Sunday morning you broadcast it the best that you can.

But what happens? Look at verse 4. "Some seed fell on the path, and the birds came and ate it up." Path? What is a path doing in the middle of a farmer's field? In those days, instead of interstate highways laid out by surveyors, there were paths that wound their way across the countryside and often meandered through fields. If you were broadcasting, some seed would fall on the path. The path is hard, packed by feet walking on it day after day. The seed is lying on the path, as if the path were a dinner plate, and the birds come and eat it up.

In verse 15, Mark says some people are like seeds on the path. When the word is sown, Satan comes and takes the word away. Sure enough, we see this when we turn to chapter 8, verse 27.

[Pause while people turn to the passage.]

Mark says Jesus and his disciples are on the way. But in Greek, the word translated "path" and the word translated "way" are the same. They are near Caesarea Philippi. In response to Jesus' question, Peter declares that Jesus is the Christ. According to verse 32, to be the Christ is to suffer, be rejected, be killed, and rise again on the third day. Furthermore, according to verse 34, Jesus declares, "If any want to become my followers, let them deny themselves and take up their cross and follow me."

Do you remember what Peter does? Peter pulls Jesus into the little room off the chancel where they control the lights and the sound system, and Peter begins to rebuke Jesus. Peter wants the glitz and the glamor. He wants to sing "Christ the Lord Is Risen Today" with trumpets. If he had been a baby boomer, he would have wanted bright lights and a rock band with an endless supply of upbeat music. But as soon as the organist begins to play "O Sacred Head, Now Wounded," he says to himself, "I didn't join the church for this."

Jesus says to him, "Get behind me, *Satan.*" How many have you lost from your congregation because the soil is hard, and the Satans in our culture come and pluck up the seed?

Let us return to verses 5–6 of the parable.

[Pause while people turn back to chapter 4.]

"Other seed fell on rocky ground where it did not have much soil, and it sprang up quickly, since it had no depth of soil. And when the sun rose, it was scorched; and since it had no root, it withered away." Rocky ground. In some places in Palestine there is a layer of limestone just beneath the surface of the soil. The seed shoots down roots. But soon the roots hit the limestone where there's no water, and the plant is scorched. Can you feel it, this seed? Right above the rock. Under the heat, it is cooking dry. Literally dying of thirst.

Mark explains this rocky ground in verses 16–17. "And these are the ones sown on rocky ground: when they hear the word, they immediately receive it with joy. But they have no root, and endure only for a while; then, when trouble or persecution arises on account of the word, immediately they fall away." Sure enough, we see this when we look at Mark 14:50.

[Pause while people turn to the passage.]

Jesus is being arrested in the garden. Judas comes with a crowd that is carrying swords and clubs. "All of [his disciples] deserted him and fled." Imagine that. They have been with Jesus for fourteen chapters. He has taken them aside privately, time after time, for encouragement, for tutorials, for prayer meetings. But when things get tough, they flee.

In the wake of the 1992 uprising in Los Angeles, two local pastors—European American and African American—get together. We need to do something, they decide. What can we do? We can have a service together to demonstrate our intention to respond to God's love for all. The night comes. The church is full—350 African Americans, 14 European Americans. And neither pastor knows what to say to the other.

We return to the parable at verse 7. "Other seed fell

among thorns, and the thorns grew up and choked it, and it yielded no grain." The bigger, tougher plants get in the way and choke it. "These are the ones who hear the word, but the cares of the world, and the lure of wealth, and the desire for other things come in and choke the word, and it yields nothing."

Who can forget the rich man in chapter 10, verse 21. Let's look at the passage.

[Pause while people turn to the passage.]

"Good Teacher, what must I do to inherit eternal life?" the man asks Jesus. A brief exchange follows. Then the text says, "Jesus loved him." Have you ever noticed how few times the Gospels say directly that Jesus loves someone? But here it is. Jesus says, "You lack one thing; go, sell what you own, and give the money to the poor, and you will have treasure in heaven; then come, follow me." Not a bad return on your investment, eternal life. But when the rich person hears this, he turns away. Can you feel the poignance of verse 22: "He was shocked and went away grieving, for he had many possessions." Don't you grieve for him, and for the ones you have lost, because the thorns have choked them out?

I try to make a clear statement of the purpose of the relationship of the parable to the setting in Mark's day and to our own setting. The vignettes that follow are provided as points of identification for pastors.

Why was this parable important enough for Mark to include it in the gospel story? This is a parable for a church that is discouraged, beaten down, tired, afraid, wondering what has happened to all the seed it has sown over the years. This is a parable for pastors like me and like you.

You put your heart and soul into a sermon. You take a prophetic stand. You put your flak jacket underneath your robe to absorb possible hits from parishioners. You're standing at the door after the service, waiting to take the hit. But one after another they file out, that good-old-boy smile on their faces, or smelling of lilac toilet water. "Nice sermon, pastor." "Nice sermon, pastor." "Nice sermon, pastor." And you wonder if they didn't stuff the little crackers that you use for the Lord's Supper in their ears. Sooner or later you ask yourself, What's the point?

The board meeting gets hot. And as soon as it is over, you drive to the house of the man who wouldn't even look you in the face when the meeting was over. You ring the bell. You don't think you need to because your heart is pounding so loudly. But he won't even open the screen door. Yet he's been in your Wednesday night Bible class for five years.

That young family with whom you've spent so much time. Where are they today? Must be out of town, visiting their family in Illinois. Kids are probably sick this week. I think she won a trip for her sales record. Must be working on their new deck. And then one day you get a postcard from that new church on the edge of town, the one with the big youth program. "The Jones family has transferred its membership to our congregation. Would you please adjust your records accordingly."

You do everything you learned to do in seminary and sometimes it feels like you get so little to grow. But just then Jesus taps you on the shoulder and whispers in your ear, "Other seed fell into good soil, and brought forth grain, growing up and increasing and yielding thirty, sixty, and a hundredfold."

Following the movement of the parable itself, the sermon formally articulates the main teaching of the parable and its allegorical interpretation only at the end of the sermon. The story of Dan Wakefield is intended to provide a strong, positive image of the harvest. It is designed to help the listeners leave the sermon encouraged for their ministries.

Lately I've been reading Dan Wakefield. He grew up in Indianapolis and one of his novels, *Going All the Way,* is set in the neighborhood where we live. It is about two young men, constantly on the search for a place to flex their muscles, for fast women, for beer, and sex. But after a while, they think plaintively that life ought to be more than women, beer, and sex."[1] The novel turns out to be a kind of description of Wakefield's life: growing up, a career in writing, enormous success, a novel made into a movie. But all along he experiences interior doubt, failed relationships, fear. In a later book, Wakefield reflects on his life:

> One balmy spring morning in Hollywood . . . I woke up screaming. I got out of bed, went into the next room, sat down on a couch, and screamed again. This was not . . . one of those waking nightmares left over from sleep that is dispelled by the comforting light of day. It was, rather, a response to the reality that another morning had broken . . . in a life I could only deal with sedated by wine, loud noise, moving images, and wired to electronic games that further distracted my fragmented attention from a growing sense of blank, nameless pain in the pit of my very being."[2]

After a difficult period of drying out, he's with a group of friends on Christmas Eve. One of them remarks that he'd like to go to mass somewhere that night. Something stirs in Wakefield, and he thinks, "I'd like to do that, too."[3]

So he looks in the newspaper and selects a Unitarian congregation in the neighborhood because it seems the least threatening. The sermon contains a line that seems to speak directly to him. He shrinks down in his pew, literally beginning to shiver, "at first from what I thought was only embarrassment at being singled out for personal attention, and discomfort at being in alien surroundings. It turned out that I had a temperature of 102."[4]

He did not return to church immediately, but the seed had broken open. After Easter, he began to attend sporadically, and Sunday by Sunday the seed tentatively began to extend its tendrils into his heart and soul. "Going to church, even belonging to it, did not solve life's problems . . . but it gave me a sense of living in a larger context, of being part of something greater than I could see through the tunnel vision of my personal concerns. . . . [W]hatever I was getting from church on Sunday mornings, I wanted more. I experienced . . . a thirst for God."[5]

Years before when Wakefield was a child, someone had planted some seeds in a moldy church basement Sunday school room in our neighborhood. If you had looked in that room, at that teacher in the plain plaid dress and those squirming whispering kids, would you have seen it? Would you have seen the seed dropping down into the soil of a child's life where it would lie for most of a life before sprouting? Would you have seen it? But it is now a harvest of thirty-fold, sixtyfold, a hundredfold.

5

Tips for Keeping
the Sermon Interesting

The purpose of the sermon is to proclaim the good news of God in such a way that the congregation will turn their lives around and live in trust (Mark 1:14–15). The best thing a preacher can do to keep a sermon interesting is to remain fixed on that purpose. A sermon may capture the listeners' interest in various ways. At least a few people delight in learning new and unexpected things about the Bible or about the ancient world. Many will perk up when the preacher says something of contemporary relevance. But interest will be at a peak when the preacher's words have the ring of life-changing good news.

The good news, however, must be expressed in human language, and some ways of speaking have more potential for being heard than others. Two different people may sing the same song, one an accomplished musician, the other not. On occasion, the song may captivate the listeners regardless of the singer's musical skill, because they know the singer and the experience that puts the song in her heart. But most often, the song will be heard and remembered when the singer has studied music and learned as much as she can about how to give voice to the song in her heart. The same is true for preaching.

So what can we preachers do to capture and hold our listeners' attention when we are preaching in the mode of commentary to give the congregation good opportunities to hear the good news? In this chapter we consider some practical things that preachers can do to help the congregation participate as fully as possible in the sermon. We illustrate with reference to the sermons in the previous chapter.

BIBLES FROM HOME

The congregation's participation in the sermon will often be enriched if the preacher invites the people to bring their Bibles from home and follow parts of the text and its exposition. When the text is open before the congregation, the visual medium of print reinforces the words of the text that the congregation otherwise only hears. The preacher can have the congregation give careful attention to particular words, grammatical constructions, figures of speech, and literary relationships within the passage and between passages. Looking at the text may cause the members of the congregation to raise their own questions, to see things in the text they have not imagined before, and even to begin to formulate their own fresh interpretations of the passage. For instance, Ron Allen asks the congregation to make use of their Bibles in his sermon on the parable of the sower and its allegorical interpretation in Mark 4.

It is best for members of the congregation to bring Bibles from home because these are the copies of the text that they are mostly likely to use from day to day. Working with a text on Sunday might encourage people to continue to meditate on the text during the week. Occasionally, people will make notes in the margins of their Bibles. Furthermore, people often develop an unspoken empathy with their particular copy of the Bible—not only the translation to which they most often turn, but the format in which it is most familiar and the copy that is familiar to their own touch. At its best, the use of the Bible in worship can help the church overcome the problem of biblical illiteracy.

Many members of long-established denominations will need to be socialized into bringing their Bibles to worship. Indeed, some members of these churches have a slightly negative view of carrying a Bible to church on Sunday. We have even heard thoughtful people in these churches refer to persons in newer movements who bring their Bibles to worship as "Bible thumpers." The preacher may need to help some of today's church members develop a positive attitude toward carrying and using the Bible.

Of course, sanctuaries should be equipped with pew Bibles so that persons who did not bring their own Bibles can have access to the material. Churches that do not have Bibles in the pews can print the passage under consideration in the worship bulletin.

This principle is not absolute. As we note in connection with the section on speaking the sermon toward the end of this chapter, some sermons call for full, immediate, and sustained face-to-face contact between preacher and congregation. Glancing back and forth between a Bible and the preacher could interfere with the encounter with the gospel. Consequently, when preaching such a sermon, the preacher who usually asks the congregation to open their Bibles and turn to the passage under consideration may need to cue the congregation to leave their Bibles closed.

The preacher who asks the congregation to use their Bibles during the sermon needs to be careful not to call the congregation's attention to the written text in such a way that it is perfunctory or boring. The preacher also needs to avoid discussions that are so technical that the congregation has difficulty following. And the preacher wants to avoid bibliolatry, that is, using the Bible in such a way that it becomes a functional idol. Indeed, the very familiarity with one's own copy of the Bible that we lauded above can become an insulation against some of the Bible's more pointed insights, calls, and challenges.

LIVELY EMBODIMENT

A key concept is in the word *embody*. For a sermon to be life-enriching good news, it must come to expression through the entire being of the preaching: clear thinking connected to strong feeling brought to expression with the voice and body in the pulpit in ways that are continuous with the personhood of the preacher and the content of the message. The more the sermon connects with the embodied living of the congregation, the clearer it will be to the listeners how the gospel can impact their everyday worlds.

Because of the emphasis on biblical exposition when preaching verse by verse, the preacher can easily, and unintentionally, envision the sermon as passing on information about the Bible in a removed way. The preacher may even slip into a dry, lecture-like mode. Preachers need to be clear that the exposition is not for its own sake, but is helping the congregation enter the world of the life-empowering gospel through the Bible. The preacher's presence in the pulpit needs to incarnate the passion and possibilities for transformation that inhere in the text and in the sermon.

How then do we embody the good news? First, the words that we choose will be the language of the body: descriptive, colorful, evocative (without being sensational), full of images, analogies, and stories from everyday experience. Second, our way of speaking—our delivery in words and body language—will be full and rich. Spoken words are more than content. They are charged with the voice and expressed in facial expression, gesture, and posture. Good delivery is natural to us in everyday situations. When we have something joyful or sad to tell, our entire body gets into the act. In order to speak as effectively in public, a preacher may need to study and practice to work through the anxieties and self-consciousness that sometimes limit our freedom of expression in the pulpit.

STORIES

Let us turn now to the verbal content of the sermon, our words apart from how we speak them. This task is easy in a book, since in the medium of print all we have is the wording of the sermon and not the manner of the pastor's presence in the act of preaching. Here we catalogue some elements of language that help the congregation participate in the sermon. The reader can see how we use these elements in the printed sermons in chapter 4 and can judge the degree to which our theory is consistent with our practice.

A story in a sermon functions in multiple ways to help the congregation participate in the sermon. A good story attracts the interest of the community. It illustrates a preacher's concern. It creates a world into which the congregation enters. In the story-world, they imaginatively experience life from the perspective of the story. In a sense, they can try on life from the perspective of the narrative. When the sermon is running commentary, a story can add interest. It can help the congregation imaginatively experience life in the world of the Bible. It can help lead the congregation to envision how their day-to-day lives can be as a result of the action of God at the center of the text and the sermon. When telling a story, the preacher can often see and feel the congregation become more involved in the sermon than they had been. Sometimes people actually lean forward.

Our sample sermons contain three kinds of stories: biblical stories retold, stories from literature, and stories from contemporary life. In his sermon on Genesis 28, Ron Allen retells the biblical story of Jacob fleeing his brother Esau after cheating him out of his father's blessing and his birthright. He retells the biblical narrative in the terms of current Western culture. Jacob is toting new, lightweight suitcases, driving the interstate looking for the cheapest gas. He draws out the episode of looking for gas into a brief plot. This modern incident of travel makes it possible for a congregation to connect with Jacob, especially with his feeling of discouragement. After a brief interlude reminding the congregation what had happened between Jacob and Esau that made this flight necessary, Ron returns to Jacob's journey, continuing in twentieth-century terms. The language is intended to help the listeners connect Jacob's experience with their own, to imagine his feelings on the basis of their own.

Linda Milavec also retells a biblical story using a modern analogy. Employing a description of Martha that she found in her study of the passage, Linda portrays Martha as a "pot-banger." The setting is a contemporary kitchen equipped with metal pots, a stove full of dishes, and a sink full of soapsuds. She draws out a brief drama of Martha's developing irritation that explodes in the hot words to Jesus found in her mouth in Luke's text. The drama and the modern setting help listeners identify with Martha.

In the sermon on the parable of the sower and its allegorical explanation in Mark 4, Ron Allen retells the story of a novel, *Going All the Way,* by Dan Wakefield, in vivid, concrete terms that are

intended to help the community connect the sermon with the concrete reality of their own embodied lives. An additional source of
interest for Ron's listeners is that the novel is set in the neighborhood in Indianapolis in which the sermon was preached.

Our sample sermons contain several stories from a third source:
the experiences of preachers themselves or of people known to
them. Linda Milavec tells the story of Susan, who hears the voice
of a gracious God telling her that she is acceptable to God just as
she is, apart from all her accomplishments. Reduced to this descriptive clause, the experience of Susan has little impact. But by
setting Susan in a grocery store, on a high emotional plane because
of all the money she is going to save as she sorts through her
coupons, God's gracious words address a concrete experience.

We find this same kind of storytelling in the Bible. Such memorable gems as "God is spirit, and those who worship [God] must
worship in spirit and in truth" (John 4:24), and "I am the resurrection and the life" (John 11:25) are words spoken by Jesus to persons in concrete circumstances. Oddly, instead of limiting their
application to the experiences of the characters in the stories, the
concreteness makes the stories available to a wide audience who
readily find in the details of the stories similarities or analogies to
their own lives.

Gil Bartholomew opens his sermon on Revelation 8 with the
story of Forrest. Forrest's story is repeated a thousand times a day.
In fact, this story began when Gil connected the example of a doctor's diagnosis of terminal illness with John the Seer's words about
Roman (and perhaps contemporary) civilization. Gil first developed the analogy in general terms of what many people experience.
But in the process of preparing the message, Gil changed that part
of the sermon to a story about a person named Forrest. This indi-
vidualizing results in a more vivid story.

In his sermon on Jacob in Genesis 28, Ron Allen relates three
incidents from his own experience: one about people he saw in
Zambia, another about a violinist, and a third about a person with
AIDS. As Ron tells these stories, he is not in a rush to get to the
point. Within the framework of meaning he is in the process of developing, the experience of the stories themselves is a significant

dimension of their meaning. Ron's vivid descriptions (toothless, faces wrinkled, bodies emaciated, surging energy, passion, fire, night sweats, cancer sores, one piece of life after another falling away) draws us into the story-world. His use of direct discourse ("How did they get that way?" "They live in an area where they grow sugar") enables us to hear people speaking to each other. We feel in our bodies the impact on others when we grab, or the joyful music of being lost and then found, or the comfort of love when we are the least lovable, even to ourselves.

DESCRIPTIVE, COLORFUL, EVOCATIVE LANGUAGE

As we have described the stories in our sample sermons and reflected on their intended impact on the congregation, we have called attention to the use of descriptive, colorful, even evocative language. Graphic words, phrases, and sentences can help the sermon come alive in the minds and hearts of the congregation. Such speech is often natural to stories, but we can use it in contexts other than narratives. Of course, a preacher needs to be careful not to use vivid language in such a way that the language calls attention to itself and thereby distracts the congregation from following the forward movement of the sermon.

In his sermon on the transfiguration of Jesus, Gil Bartholomew enumerates various ways we deal with significant challenges in our lives. One of the ways is that "we simply retreat to the quiet moment stolen from dark nights or early dawns." This language does more than name two times when we size up things. "Dark nights" and "early dawns" summon feelings of sleepless tossing and turning from the depths of our half-forgotten past. The word "retreat" carries a sense of rest from struggle, and the word "stolen" calls forth the tension of wrestling with something that seems not to belong to us. Later in the sermon, Gil draws us into the experience of Peter, John, and James as they enter the cloud: "a damp, gray, depressing mist envelops them." These words, not in Luke's text, create the feel of what it is like to be enshrouded by a cloud.

In Ron Allen's sermon on the parable of the sower in Mark 4, he expands Mark's images of what could happen to seed when sown by a farmer in first-century Palestine. Mark's language is like a sketch, Ron's like a photograph. Ron simply describes the practice of sowing in Mark's day, using information he got from a Bible dictionary. Mark did not need to show a full-color photo of sowing seed to his audience. He could provide an outline, and they could color it for themselves. When that is possible, it is better for the listeners. First, each listener is free to continue to bring to the outline her or his own experience. Second, it is helpful when a storyteller or a preacher helps the congregation make their own contributions to finding meaning in the sermon.

When, however, the sketches are from a world that is foreign to the listeners, they are not positioned to fill in the details. So in his sermon, Ron helps his twentieth-century listener color Mark's sketch the way Mark's original listeners would have: "A peasant in a rough woven shirt. A bag of seed wrapped around the waist. Taking a handful of seed from the bag and with a practiced movement broadcasting it over the field." Mark does not spell out this picture in detail. It is essential to the parable, and not to be taken for granted among current listeners.

ANALOGIES AND METAPHORS

Another treasury of verbal riches for embodying the good news is the wealth of analogies and metaphors available from everyday life. Daily language is full of these figures of speech. When using these kinds of language, we speak of one thing in order to help our listeners understand something else. An analogy is a simple comparison. Metaphor speaks of something familiar in an unfamiliar way in order to provoke the listener to perceive the familiar in a fresh way. Analogies and metaphors can be as brief as a phrase or as long as a story.

In Gil Bartholomew's sermon on the transfiguration of Jesus, he indicates the importance of Moses and Elijah by drawing an analogy between them and George Washington and Abraham Lincoln. The same preacher helps the listeners understand Revelation 8 through an analogy between John the Seer's vision and a physician's diagnosis of a terminal illness. Ron Allen uses an analogy in his sermon on Mark 4 when comparing the ancient world of Roman occupation and contemporary scenes of ethnic cleansing, tribal warfare, and social violence. The violence we connect with these places in today's society helps us get a sense of the violence of ancient Rome.

Metaphors are more complex than analogies. When they work, they do more than help us understand a foreign world with the help of something similar in our own world. They give us a powerful way of thinking about our own setting. Ron Allen uses two vivid metaphors in his sermon on Jacob and the ladder in Genesis 28. At one point, he invites us to imagine going to church on Sunday morning "feeling like a burned-out house." At another point, he pictures the prophetic preacher as putting on a flak jacket beneath a preaching robe, and waiting to take the hit. In his sermon on Mark 4, the metaphors are more complex. Ron begins with the Bible's own metaphor of the ancient way of sowing seed as a way of speaking of the religious life. Then he moves to Jesus' own explanation of this powerful motif as a metaphor for sowing the "word." Then Ron makes a new metaphorical move: Still speaking of seed, he pictures it falling into the cracks between the pages of a Bible, and the reader trying to scrape it out. What an image for our efforts to understand the Bible! Next he pictures us trying to catch the seed blowing through the air—while we are watching the evening news. This is a provocative image for our efforts to hear the word in the chaos of media events. Another image Ron uses is the receiving of a seed from the clammy hand of a parishioner dying of cancer. There it is—the word—so tiny, sticking to your hand, but hard to grasp because it is so small. There it is, pasted to your palm—but what can you do with it in the face of such agony?

We find Ron's most complex metaphor in his sermon on the story of Jacob and his dream. Ron tells us that, according to normal Hebrew usage, the word that is usually translated "ladder" may more accurately be pictured as a ramp. He paints pictures of two kinds of ramps: the kind construction companies build when they are making a superhighway and handicapped accessible ramps. Then he ruminates over the second picture. "Think of that: heaven as handicapped-accessible." This vivid picture of an otherwise colorless ramp suddenly opens into a metaphor. At present, the word *handicapped* triggers in the minds of most listeners the picture of someone with a physical disability, especially when it is used to specify a type of ramp. To extend it to all people is to use it metaphorically. Would anyone listening to this sermon imagine that Ron is suggesting that special provision needs to be made for those who are somehow physically impaired? This image suggests a powerful new way of thinking about both ourselves and heaven.

SPEAKING THE SERMON

We turn now to that aspect of preaching that is sometimes called "delivery." We resist this way of speaking because it can suggest a distance in relationship between the content of the sermon and the act of preaching. In this way of speaking, the preacher has the same relationship to the sermon as the courier from the delivery service who brings a package to your house. The package is an entity in its own right. The agent simply delivers the package without becoming involved with it or with you. We prefer to think that the preacher embodies the sermon, that is, brings it to life through his or her whole being in such a way that in connects at the deepest levels with the congregation. The new sensitivity to media in communication, and the resurgence of oral storytelling during the last quarter century, open us to some new choices.

In some circles, a good preaching environment has been envisioned as a setting in which the preacher stands behind a pulpit and speaks to a congregation either with or without the aid of a manuscript or notes. In this architectural setting, our attention in regard to the act of speaking is focused on voice quality, facial expression, eye contact, posture, and gesture, particularly from the chest up as the preacher stands in one location.

This setting encourages a particular medium of sermon preparation and communication. The pulpit encourages writing and reading by providing a place to lay a written manuscript or notes. When preachers attend to the fact that the pulpit is a historic symbol of the importance of the interpretation of the gospel in the community, and when they do not simply read the sermon, this setting can be an effective way of communicating the gospel. A good preacher speaks a message that flows from her or his own heart. These preachers are fully present to the congregation, and use notes or manuscript to do nothing more than jog the memory or keep the sermon on track. However, preachers sometimes have a tendency to read the sermon without making contact with the congregation, or to lean on the pulpit in such a way that its symbolism is bypassed. Even those who memorize their sermons sometimes speak them as if they are reading the sermon like a ticker tape from their minds. In some circumstances, the pulpit effectively comes between the preacher and the listeners.

Furthermore, most pulpits hide a good bit of the preacher's body. Fortress-like pulpits discourage movement while the minister is preaching. The manuscript has a tendency to become the sermon. Indeed, some preachers could substitute a tape recorder for their own voice and body with little loss.

The widespread revival of the art of storytelling alerts us to a significant alternative that can help some preachers help their congregations encounter the gospel. The storyteller frequently tells a story, from memory, while standing freely in the midst of a group. The preacher, likewise, might speak the sermon by leaving the pulpit and standing in the chancel. The preacher develops the sermon in a way that makes it easier to remember. Without a pulpit to restrict movement, and free of a bundle of notes, the preacher is present to the community with the whole body unrestricted, and free to shape space.

While this kind of delivery raises fears that preaching will be theatrical, it can be a most natural form of human communication. It builds on the fact that in many situations of human interaction, there is no physical object between the persons who are speaking with one another. Immediacy of communication can result.

For example, when Linda Milavec retold the story of Martha and Mary, she moved about the chancel area. She spoke about each character in a different part of the chancel. She freely expressed the words of each character with her whole body, the way people do in normal conversation.

Linda Milavec offers some extended comments about the way she played out her text in the medium of memory and body language, and how that is a decidedly different medium from a sermon delivered from behind a pulpit. Her comments make clear that oral structuring and verse by verse preaching can go hand in hand. Her comments also deal with questions frequently asked by pastors who do not yet feel the courage to move from behind the pulpit and away from their texts: "How can I remember it all? What if I leave out something? What if I freeze?"

Being able to deliver an oral sermon with passion and energy has much to do with organizing several different memorable units into a whole. The preaching event begins with the learning of the story by heart. Find its twists and turns and surprises. Let it bubble around inside you for the entire preparation time. Let it intersect with your conversations, with the news you hear, the television you watch, the events you see going on around you. Dive into the trouble spots, the boring spots, the places that don't make sense. These will be the key to bringing the text alive for an audience who is essentially cold to the story.

Once the story starts to come alive for you (and perhaps a small community of learners with you), you are ready to extend into the actual construction of a sermon. An oral sermon is more about finding a number of stories within one story than about exposition of an idea. One way to do this is to divide a piece of paper into several big blocks, each containing a few key words or images. During the preparation time sometimes the blocks themselves will change as one listens for the surprise and tension of the text.

For the sermon on Martha and Mary, eight blocks could be included: (1) Introduction. Men and women are different. Women trained to be different with pink booties, trained to be nice, giving themselves over—but what about recognition? (2) Jesus and the disciples on the way. They stop at the house of Martha. (3) What do we know about Martha? A woman of substance. Bold. Practical. A Pot-banger. (4) Martha the hospitality maker as contrasted with her out-of-line sister. Martha's challenge (hands on hips). The disciples agree. (5) Every woman since the invention of pink booties is now listening. He had better get it right. (6) Jesus' challenge back. (7) Jesus is on to a different God. Susan's story (punch line: "You don't have to impress me."). (8) Mary has chosen the better part. What has Mary chosen? What are the implications for Martha? For us? For Susan's story?

This preacher's experience of trying to stay within a twenty-minute sermon suggests that any more than eight blocks will either be too cumbersome, or will not allow for the richness of each unit to have the leisure to sparkle with color or surprise. Sometimes even using colors or line drawings to help remember the different blocks helps lodge them in the preacher's mind. Once the blocks seem somewhat full, and yet not so complex that they cannot be easily spoken, blocking the text spacewise in the center of the preaching area itself will let the flow of the text be remembered in your body as well as mind, which is the storyteller's key to being relaxed and confident within an oral sermon.

Having an opening line or story and a clear closing image or statement that you are excited about will also help you to work freely and energetically as you preach. Before the actual delivery this preacher finds it helpful to move quickly through the opening, the blocks themselves, and the ending, much as one sees the Olympic luge runners at the top of the hill before they begin their thrilling yet frightening descent. Notice the way they close their eyes, moving their heads through the whole course. Gathering the anxiety and the thrill of being able to present *good news* invites the same inner preparation. By the time of the actual delivery, you may have been over the text thirty times. You may have tried it out on your cat, your dog, your goldfish, your mirror, your mailman, and anyone next to you in the car. The anxiety of the actual moment before delivery is a blessing. Be more worried if you do not feel a certain anxiety.

By the actual time of the sermon's delivery, it is important to say in one line its direction and its message. This one phrase or one line does not necessarily need to be the sermon title (you may want to save the punch line), but it guides the teller throughout the several blocks toward the richly experienced "truth" that the hearers hopefully will also experience in their hearts and minds. While constructing the sermon the preacher needs to stay open to the struggle within himself or herself that makes this particular piece of good news difficult to live into. Knowing and being vulnerable with our own spiritual struggles, as well as in the vulnerability of this delivery style, allows the listeners to hear themselves in the struggle and to be addressed in the good news.

A minor variation on preaching from a place other than the pulpit can also help with memory. A preacher can often carry a small, unobtrusive Bible in one hand. Typically, all it takes is a glance at the biblical text itself for the well-prepared preacher to remember what comes next in the sermon.

In a book on the oral reading of scripture, Charlotte Lee has pointed out that this way of speaking sets up sympathetic responses in the bodies of the listeners. The congregation does more than hear the preacher's words. They experience the characters' feelings in their own muscles and viscera.[1] This kind of reception for a sermon is not only more powerful, and therefore more memorable, it is more true to the fullness of life.

We are not suggesting that all preachers leave the pulpit every Sunday. Some sermons and occasions call for the symbolism of the pulpit. However, other sermons and occasions can be well served by the alternative pattern of bringing the sermon to life that we have just described. The preacher does not leave the pulpit for the sake of leaving the pulpit, or of winning accolades from the congregation for preaching without notes. The preacher leaves the pulpit when it enhances the congregation's encounter with the text.

6

Occasions for Preaching
Verse by Verse

The homiletics revival of the last generation has called forth a multitude of possibilities for the form, movement, and function of the sermon.[1] One of the preacher's responsibilities is to locate (or create) a genre and content for the sermon that is fitting for each occasion and community. A congregation that has just experienced a moment in which eschatological reality has appeared in the midst of the community's life may need nothing more than to celebrate God's presence and power through the telling of stories. A congregation in the midst of agonizing conflict over an ethical issue may need to make its patient way through logical, critical analysis of the various positions on and dimensions of the issue. Through priestly listening, the preacher plots the intersection of congregational needs and Christian resources.[2]

When does the preacher turn to running commentary? No magical formula can answer this question. The decision of what and how to preach on a given Sunday nearly always combines an amalgam that includes self-conscious critical correlation of the situation of the community with the resources of the gospel as well as the pastor's own hunches, intuitions, and feelings. Factors beyond the preacher's control (or awareness) cause some thoughtfully designed sermons to die even as they are spoken; on the other hand, other factors can help some sermons that should be stillborn cry with life. Nonetheless, some occasions or needs are often especially suited to running commentary. This chapter brings nine such occasions into view.

WHEN A BIBLICAL PASSAGE CORRELATES
WITH THE SITUATION OF THE CONGREGATION

Specific biblical passages often articulate perspectives that a congregation needs to encounter in order to maintain a strong, healthy theological outlook, identity, and mission. Specific passages can help the congregation enlarge, supplement, correct, or intensify aspects of its life (e.g., vision, feeling, or behavior). Running commentary provides a means whereby the community can connect with the pertinent passage(s) with directness and depth.

From time to time, for instance, nearly every congregation in the United States needs to be reminded of the heart of Christian faith: justification by grace through faith. North American culture, with its emphasis on productivity as a measure of worth, is a fertile breeding ground for works righteousness. When works righteousness begins to show itself in a congregation (perhaps subtly), the preacher could work word by word through Romans 3:21–31 or Ephesians 2:1–10. The preacher would have maximum opportunity to help the congregation rediscover (or discover) the unmerited love of God as the ground of its being and, further, to understand the cosmic dimensions of this grace.

When a community is in grief, it needs to work through its grief in a way that both acknowledges the pain of its situation and that frames its situation in faith. A communal lament from the Psalms may provide just such an occasion, as the genre of communal lament contains the following elements: (1) invocation of the divine presence, (2) explanation of the community's complaint, (3) confession of trust in God, (4) supplication for help (or forgiveness). As Walter Brueggemann says, such psalms provide a form for dealing with grief.[3] Psalm 44 supplies such a form for a community in distress as it moves from invocation (vv. 1–8) through explanation of its complaint (vv. 9–16) and confession of trust in God (vv. 17–22) to supplication (vv. 23–26). The preacher could work through the psalm segment by segment, correlating the feelings, thoughts, and needs of the congregation with each segment.

Conflict sometimes develops in Christian communities. In such a case, a pastor might find an ideal base from which to enter into the community's life in Matthew 5:21–26, with its process for moving from alienation to reconciliation. A sequential exposition of the text could clarify its meaning (especially the surprising admonition, "If you remember that your brother or sister has something against you") and help the congregation understand its situation and the next necessary steps toward resolving the conflict.

WHEN PREACHING CONTINUOUSLY
THROUGH A BOOK OF THE BIBLE

A congregation may profit from working systematically through a book of the Bible. This benefit may result directly from a congregation's need. For instance, a community that is fearful because of radical changes in its world might be encouraged by a systematic encounter with Isaiah 40–55 and its ministry to a community in exile. The benefit may also result from concerns that have less existential urgency. A congregation that has decided to expand its knowledge of the Bible might begin by following the stories of Genesis.

This pattern is called *lectio continua* (continuous reading). It was in use in the synagogue by the time of Jesus. In chapter 2 we noted its presence at Qumran and in the midrashim. It has been a staple in Christian preaching at significant moments since the time of Origen, and was especially important in the Reformation.[4] It can be a part of lectionary preaching (as noted in our discussion of the Revised Common Lectionary below), or the pastor can freely choose to adopt it.

Hughes Oliphant Old, a pastor in the Presbyterian Church (U.S.A.), has used *lectio continua* as the basis for many years for preaching. He writes:

> How did the congregation feel about my preaching methods? Well, knowing how the faithful blow hot and cold in evaluating their *dominie,* I am slow to make too many claims about people's reactions to my labors. One hard fact I can produce, however, is that when the congregation went looking for my successor, they looked for someone who would use the lectio continua approach to preaching.[5]

Old adapted the pattern of the Reformers by choosing representative texts (rarely preaching more than a dozen sermons on a single book). He planned his series so that they coordinated with the seasons of the Christian year (for example, preaching on Matthew's stories of the nativity in Advent and Christmas). In a year he would be careful to turn to many different types of biblical literature and always include "a major series on a Gospel, a major series on another New Testament book, and a major series on an Old Testament book."[6] Along the way, he tried to keep the selection of texts and the directions of the sermons in touch with congregational needs.

The Revised Common Lectionary offers opportunities for this pattern of preaching.[7] For most of the special seasons and days (Advent, Christmas, Epiphany Day, Lent, Easter, Pentecost Day), the Revised Common Lectionary follows the principle of *lectio selecta*. The readings from the Bible are selected to illumine the theological motifs of the season. For instance, in Advent the readings point to the coming of God through Christ. The Revised Common Lectionary is divided into a three-year cycle, with Year A focusing on Matthew, Year B on Mark, and Year C on Luke. During the special seasons, readings from the Fourth Gospel appear from time to time. However, in the special seasons the readings from the Gospels are selected for the theological purpose they perform on each Sunday; from one Sunday to another, the Gospel readings are not related to one another by means of their literary connection in the narratives. Each Sunday, the other readings (First Testament, epistle, psalm) are intended to relate to the Gospel reading; these supportive readings do not relate with one another from one Sunday to the next. A sermon can take the form of running commentary on any passage on any given Sunday, but the commentary would seldom be connected sequentially with the readings on the previous or following Sundays.

In Ordinary Time (the Sundays after Epiphany and after Pentecost) the Gospel readings in the Revised Common Lectionary follow the pattern of *lectio continua*. Thus, in Year A, one can follow Matthew, in Year B, Mark, and in Year C, Luke. During this same period, the epistle readings are also continuous. In the Sundays after Epiphany in all three years, 1 Corinthians is highlighted. On the Sundays after Pentecost in Year A, the congregation reads through representative passages from Romans, Philippians, and 1 Thessalonians. In Year B, the serial epistle selections are from 2 Corinthians, Ephesians, James, and Hebrews. In Year C, the readings come from Galatians, Colossians, Hebrews, 1 and 2 Timothy, and 2 Thessalonians. Any of these sequences would be an excellent basis for a series of *lectio continua* sermons in the style of running commentary.

The Revised Common Lectionary furnishes two sets of readings from the First Testament for each Sunday in Ordinary Time after Pentecost. Each set contains a psalm and another passage from the First Testament. One set coordinates with the Gospel text. The other set represents major bodies of literature in the First Testament. In Year A, the passages trace ancestral stories in Genesis and Exodus with supplements from Deuteronomy, Joshua, and Judges. Year B focuses on 1 and 2 Samuel and 1 and 2 Kings as well as the wisdom literature and Ruth. Year C brings 1 and 2 Kings (with emphasis on the prophets) and the prophetic corpus. Some of these passages from the First Testament follow one another closely in the books or corpora in which they are found, so that one could preach from one Sunday to the next in the pattern of *lectio continua*. Frequently, however, the lectionary omits significant amounts of biblical material between the pericopes; the connection from one Sunday to the next is lost. Of course, any text can be preached in the mode of running commentary, but when the readings do not relate closely to one another, the force of building from one Sunday to the next may be lost. The pastor who wishes to preach continuously from the books of the First Testament may sometimes find it advantageous to abandon the lectionary (or to supplement the lectionary readings) for a period.

A qualification is in order. As noted by Hughes Oliphant Old, the pastor may want to select representative texts from a biblical book (or corpus) as the basis for preaching. The congregation may weary of a biblical book. In order to help maintain the congregation's interest, the preacher might select key texts for detailed exposition. The pastor could summarize the biblical material that is found between the pivotal texts so that the congregation has a sense of the context of the pivotal passages.

WHEN THE CONGREGATION HAS QUESTIONS ABOUT BIBLICAL PASSAGES OR ABOUT METHODS OF BIBLICAL INTERPRETATION

A congregation (or some members of a congregation) sometimes have questions about the possible meanings of particular biblical passages. Running commentary can serve as a significant venue into the heart of these questions and texts. For example, during a time of war (or threat of war), the Christian community is likely to be curious about passages in the Bible that picture God as a warrior, or Israel as participating in a holy war with divine approval. What sense does the community make of such passages in the light of its understanding of God's universal love and God's universal call for justice? Does the congregation experience a contradiction between the nation's call to arms and sacred passages such as "You shall not murder [or kill]" (Ex. 20:13) or the pericope that contains, "Love your enemies and pray for those who persecute you" (Matt. 5:44)?

The congregation may also have questions about how to interpret the Bible. Curiosity often arises as believers read the Bible as a part of daily household worship. The Bible can seem obscure, strange, confusing, and even contradictory when read without the aid of a commentary or a preacher's interpretation. While reading 1 Samuel 14:36–46 in a cycle of daily Bible readings, a person or a larger household community naturally may be curious. How could Saul condemn his own son, Jonathan, to death, even when Jonathan had violated his father's oath? What are Urim and Thummim? Why did ancient people believe these objects revealed the divine will? Why don't we use Urim and Thummim to make decisions in our monthly board meetings? Running commentary could both respond to such specific queries and model how Christians might resolve such questions through use of helpful resources.

Questions also come up in response to the interpretations of the

Bible put forth by Christian communities beyond one's own. Many people become inquisitive about how to interpret the Bible when they encounter a biblical interpretation in the media or through friends and acquaintances that strikes them as unusual. For example, a television preacher takes 1 Thessalonians 4:13–5:11 (the second coming of Jesus on the clouds, accompanied by the archangel's cry, God's trumpet call, and the dead rising to meet Jesus on the clouds in the air) as a blueprint of events to come. Such texts and ideas have not been staples in the preaching and teaching of the long-established churches in recent years. Some in the congregation will ask, "Is that what Paul really means? If so, does our church believe it?" Running commentary can help a congregation discover how to respond to those questions by modeling the exegesis of the ancient text. If that mid-air scenario is what Paul intends, the sermon might move from the commentary to pertinent theological questions. Does the nonoccurrence of that event call God's faithfulness (as well as the trustworthiness of Paul and the Bible) into question? Or can we draw a positive meaning from that passage by respecting the differences between the Thessalonian worldview and our own, while probing for those intentions of the text that transcend worldview?

WHEN A TEXT IS DIFFICULT

Some texts make use of ancient vocabulary, assumptions, or practices that are hard for the contemporary congregation to understand. For example, the extended passage Exodus 25:1–31:18 describes the tabernacle. At one level, many in today's congregation will not be able to picture accurately some of the details of the tabernacle. How long is a cubit? What is acacia wood? What did the mercy seat look like? What is a calyxe? An ephod? At another level, few in today's typical congregation will innately understand the symbolism of the elements of the tabernacle as they come together to represent the world in which the Israelites lived. Running commentary could provide the information needed to understand the elements of the tabernacle, and could explore how the elements of the tabernacle (and the tabernacle as a whole) symbolized the trustworthiness of Israel's life with God. When preaching on the tabernacle in Exodus, the preacher might find it useful to provide a drawing of the tabernacle in the form of a printed handout or a projected image.

Some texts contain theological ideas that are hard for contemporary believers to fathom. For instance, why should the ceremony described in Numbers 19 (which involved slaughtering a red heifer, sprinkling its blood on the tent of meeting, and going through a series of lustral washings) be necessary to cleanse one from uncleanness that resulted from touching a corpse? To take another example, today's listener may think of *flesh* as pertaining only to the material world and *spirit* as pertaining to the nonmaterial world. Such a listener would be befuddled when reading Galatians 5:13–25, in which Paul uses these two words to refer to two domains of cosmic existence: one animated by the Spirit of God and the other operating without reference to God and God's purposes. In both passages, running commentary would be a natural vehicle to clarify the content of the texts.

Still other texts are intellectually, theologically, or morally problematic. As we noted in chapter 1, running commentary may be of particular help in these cases. For example, Joshua 8:1–29 climaxes with the destruction of Ai and all its human inhabitants. Psalm 140:9–11 prays for God to curse those who have oppressed the psalmist; God is asked to let burning coals fall on them and to let them be flung into eternal pits. In Acts 5:1–11, Ananias and Sapphira fall down dead when they are confronted about their dishonesty concerning the amount of money they have withheld from the Christian community. The seven angels in Revelation 8:1–9:20 approve of the savage destruction of vast segments of the natural world and humankind. Running commentary can also help the congregation understand why these motifs were important to communities in the ancient world but why they are difficult for today's people to endorse. Running commentary can help the congregation identify clearly the points at which these passages (and others similar to them) do not witness to God's love for all or God's will for justice for all. Other forms of preaching can accomplish these purposes as well, but continuous exposition helps the congregation comprehensively understand the detail of the difficulties in the texts.

WHEN THE PREACHER IS STRUGGLING WITH THE FORM AND MOVEMENT OF A SERMON, OR WHEN PREPARATION TIME IS SHORT

As we have seen in chapter 4, running commentary is not a wooden form; it can be expressed with variations. But its main theme is always segment by segment exposition. This form and movement can come to the aid of a preacher who is struggling with the form and movement of a sermon. Pastors sometimes accumulate significant exegetical discoveries—hermeneutical points of contact between the text and the congregation's encounter with the text. But even when a central organizing focus for the content of the sermon has become clear, the preacher is sometimes frustrated with how to put together the sermon itself. Running commentary can often step into the gap between exegetical-hermeneutical potential and sermonic form.

One of the most fervent principles of contemporary homiletical literature is that the preacher needs to begin sermon preparation early in the week so as to allow plenty of time for disciplined research and preparation as well as for the sermon to percolate in the imagination. Like chili that simmers overnight, most sermons benefit from steeping in the pastor's consciousness (and unconsciousness) for several days. As preachers live through the week, they become aware of previously unnoticed connections among the text, the sermon, and the congregation. Indeed, many pastors so appreciate the values of long-term preparation that they select preaching texts, and even themes, weeks in advance.

However, situations do sometimes arise when the time of preparation is short. A tragedy at the beginning of the week forces sermon preparation time into Friday, Saturday, or even Sunday morning. A sermon that looks promising on Monday collapses by Friday. A major public event on Thursday renders the completed

sermon impertinent. A meeting of the middle level judicatory
(e.g., Conference, District, Presbytery) occupies the first days of
the week. Running commentary can sometimes help a preacher
bring together solid biblical content, thoughtful hermeneutics, and
functional sermonic form in a limited period of time.

A word of caution is in order. The use of running commentary
under these latter circumstances requires preachers to be familiar
enough with the content of the Bible that they can determine
honorable connections between the congregation and biblical
passages. While we have earlier lamented the biblical illiteracy of
many congregations today, a correlate is that some clergy do not
have the Bible in their bones either. Hence, pastors should turn
to running commentary under the press of time only when they
are confident that they have a suitable match between text and
context. When in doubt, the preacher might turn to a topical
sermon.

ALMOST ANY SUNDAY WHEN THE
PREACHER HAS ENERGY FOR THE TEXT

The pastor does not need to be faced with a special situation in
which to preach in running commentary. This mode can serve
many Sundays when preacher and congregation gather around the
Bible in order to become more cognizant of the presence of the
transcendent. A text that is presented in the lectionary or that
otherwise comes to the pastor's awareness can bring forth energy
in the preacher. Sometimes that excitement is sufficient to captivate both preacher and congregation, provided that the energy
with the text comes at a moment when the text and community
can come together in a helpful way. Congregations often respond
positively to energy in the pulpit. Running commentary sometimes gives form to the preacher's dynamism in such a way that the
congregation can become energized as well.

Writing about teaching sermons, Thomas G. Long reminds us,
"No one teaching style will suffice to convey the totality of the
Christian gospel." Some dimensions of Christian reality can be ex-
pressed in propositions and ideas. But "there are some aspects of

the gospel that can only be taught with a hymn, or a poem, or a story. No method alone will do."[8] Running commentary may not be the approach for every sermon every Sunday. But it can take its place in the great choir of homiletical possibilities. We believe it can contribute in a significant way to the revitalization of the church in our time.

Notes

INTRODUCTION

1. In the early 1970s, fresh approaches to preaching began to appear. The revival began in part as reaction to the limitations of the older homiletical formulas, in part as response to fresh insights in human knowledge and communication, in part in response to the emergence of new forms of literary and rhetorical criticisms in biblical studies, in part in recognition of the profoundly contextual nature of each sermon, and in part in recognition that the disestablishment of Christian communities in North America calls for approaches to preaching that are suited to the new situation. For a collection of representative samples of preaching from the past and present, see *Patterns for Preaching: A Sermon Sampler*, ed. Ronald J. Allen (St. Louis: Chalice Press, 1998).

2. Fred B. Craddock, *As One without Authority* (Nashville: Abingdon Press, 1979, originally published 1971).

3. Edmund Steimle, Morris Niedenthal, and Charles Rice, *Preaching the Story* (Philadelphia: Fortress Press, 1980).

4. Eugene Lowry, *The Homiletical Plot* (Atlanta: John Knox Press, 1980).

5. Henry Mitchell, *Celebration and Experience in Preaching* (Nashville: Abingdon Press, 1990).

6. Fred B. Craddock, *Overhearing the Gospel* (Nashville: Abingdon Press, 1978).

7. David G. Buttrick, *Homiletic: Moves and Structures* (Philadelphia: Fortress Press, 1987).

8. Thomas G. Long, *Preaching and the Literary Forms of the Bible* (Philadelphia: Fortress Press, 1988); Sidney Greidanus, *The Modern Preacher and the Ancient Text: Interpreting and Preaching Biblical Literature* (Grand Rapids: Wm. B. Eerdmans Publishing Co., 1988); Don M. Wardlaw, ed., *Preaching Biblically* (Philadelphia: Fortress Press, 1983); Mike Graves, *The Sermon as Symphony: Preaching the Literary Forms of the New Testament* (Valley Forge: Judson Press, 1997); and Ronald J. Allen, *Contemporary Biblical Interpretation for Preaching* (Valley Forge: Judson Press, 1984), 49–59.

9. Paul Scott Wilson, *Imagination of the Heart: New Understandings in Preaching* (Nashville: Abingdon Press, 1988); Charles L. Rice, *Interpretation and Imagination: The Preacher and Contemporary Literature*, Preacher's Paperback Library (Philadelphia: Fortress Press, 1970).

10. Thomas H. Troeger, *Imagining the Sermon* (Nashville: Abingdon Press, 1990).

11. Clyde E. Fant, *Preaching for Today*, rev. ed. (San Francisco: Harper and Row Publishers, 1987); Richard F. Ward, *Speaking from the Heart: Preaching with Passion* (Nashville: Abingdon Press, 1992).

12. Ronald J. Allen, *Interpreting the Gospel: An Introduction to Preaching* (St. Louis: Chalice Press, 1998), 299, n. 2; John S. McClure, *The Roundtable Pulpit: Collaborative Preaching* (Nashville: Abingdon Press, 1995); Lucy Atkinson Rose, *Sharing the Word: Preaching in the Roundtable Church* (Louisville, Ky.: Westminster John Knox Press, 1997).

13. Ronald J. Allen, *Preaching the Topical Sermon* (Louisville, Ky.: Westminster/ John Knox Press, 1992), cf. Buttrick, *Homiletic,* 405–488.

14. We owe this designation to Eugene L. Lowry, *How to Preach a Parable* (Nashville: Abingdon Press, 1989), who uses it to describe his own analysis of sermons that appear in *How to Preach a Parable.* To be sure, running commentary has been centerstage in the preaching of many Christian communities of evangelical and fundamental theological persuasion. For example, see John MacArthur Jr., Richard Mayhue, Robert Thomas, and The Master's Seminary Faculty and Staff, *Rediscovering Expository Preaching* (Waco, Tex.: Word Books, 1992).

15. For a brief bibliography on the classification of sermons, see Allen, *Preaching the Topical Sermon,* 146.

16. There are many different modes of biblical exposition in the pulpit. For example, see Paul Scott Wilson, *The Practice of Preaching* (Nashville: Abingdon Press, 1995); Thomas G. Long, *The Witness of Preaching* (Louisville, Ky.: Westminster/John Knox Press, 1989); Fred B. Craddock, *Preaching* (Nashville: Abingdon Press, 1985). We regard the sermon as running commentary as a subdivision of the more general category of expository preaching.

CHAPTER 1: THE ATTRACTIVENESS OF PREACHING VERSE BY VERSE

1. James Fish, "Teaching as We Preach—Education for the Sake of Mission," *Currents in Theology and Mission* 18 (1991): 357.

2. Ibid., 358.

3. Lyle Schaller, *Twenty-one Bridges to the Twenty-first Century* (Nashville: Abingdon Press, 1994), 84–85.

4. Lyle Schaller, "How Long Is the Sermon?" *The Parish Paper* 1, no. 11 (1994): 1.

5. Alexander Campbell, *Millennial Harbinger* 4 (1833): 370.

6. Schaller, *Twenty-one Bridges to the Twenty-first Century,* 84.

7. For a concise overview of current methods of biblical scholarship, see William A. Baird, "Biblical Criticism: New Testament," in *The Anchor Bible Dictionary,* ed. David Noel Freedman, et al. (Garden City, N.Y.: Doubleday, 1992), 1: 730–36. Cf. Ronald J. Allen, *Contemporary Biblical Interpretation for Preaching* (Valley Forge: Judson Press, 1984).

8. For a comprehensive bibliography on literary criticism and the Bible, see Mark Allan Powell, Cecile Gray, and Melissa Curtis, *The Bible and Modern Literary Criticism: A Critical Assessment and Annotated Bibliography,* Bibliographies and Indexes in Religious Studies, no. 22 (Westport, Conn.: Greenwood Press, 1992).

9. On suspicion, the foundational work is Paul Ricoeur, *Freud and Philosophy,* trans. Dennis Savage (New Haven, Conn: Yale University Press, 1970); on ideology, see Terry Eagleton, *Ideology* (London: Verso Publishing Co., 1991).

For examples of ideology criticism, see the essays in *Semeia* 59 (1992) and many of the writings of Walter Brueggemann.

10. For example, Werner Kelber, *The Oral and the Written Gospel* (Philadelphia: Fortress Press, 1983).

11. For biblical interpretation as an oral-aural event, the classic work is Thomas Boomershine, *Story Journey* (Nashville: Abingdon Press, 1988).

12. For guidance in the sermon as an oral-aural event, see Richard F. Ward, *Preaching with Passion* (Nashville: Abingdon Press, 1992).

13. For an examination of how scripture functions in preaching in major theological positions, see Donald K. McKim, *The Bible in Theology and Preaching* (Nashville: Abingdon Press, 1994).

14. For further comparison and contrast in the implications for preaching in the postliberal and revisionary theological camps, see Ronald J. Allen, "Two Approaches to Theology and Their Implications for Preaching," *Journal for Preachers* 19, no. 3 (1996): 38–48.

15. Stanley Hauerwas and William Willimon, *Resident Aliens* (Nashville: Abingdon Press, 1989), 24. Hauerwas's and Willimon's emphasis.

16. See the literature cited in the introduction, notes 2–10, especially 9–10.

17. For a method and criteria by which to make such an assessment, see Clark M. Williamson and Ronald J. Allen, *A Credible and Timely Word* (St. Louis: Chalice Press, 1992), 70–129.

CHAPTER 2: THE LIVELY TRADITION OF PREACHING VERSE BY VERSE

1. For examples of disciplines (especially form criticism, tradition-history, canonical criticism, and inner-biblical exegesis) that attempt to trace this process, see the literature reviewed in John Goldingay, *Approaches to Old Testament Interpretation*, updated ed. (Downers Grove, Ill.: InterVarsity Press, 1990), 123–38, 198–99. See also the concise overviews in Gerhard Hasel, *Old Testament Theology: Basic Issues in the Current Debate*, rev. and expanded ed. (Grand Rapids: Wm. B. Eerdmans Publishing Co., 1991), 28–114.

2. Goldingay, *Approaches to Old Testament Interpretation*, 132–33.

3. For literature discussing other interpretive passages in which traditions in the Hebrew Bible comment upon one another, see Goldingay, *Approaches to Old Testament Interpretation*, and Gary Porton, "Midrash," in *The Anchor Bible Dictionary*, ed. David Noel Freedman et al. (Garden City, N.Y.: Doubleday, 1992), 4:819.

4. See Rex Mason, *Preaching the Tradition: Homily and Hermeneutics after the Exile* (Cambridge: Cambridge University Press, 1990), especially pp. 257–62.

5. However, this process is not disinterested elucidation. The tradition itself is often transformed. Some elements are repressed while others are refocused and still others are added.

6. Michael Fishbane, *Biblical Interpretation in Ancient Israel* (Oxford: Clarendon Press, 1985), 1. Fishbane finds that the Old Testament contains the roots of many Jewish exegetical impulses that became fully manifest in the litera-

ture of Judaism during the Hellenistic age (circa 300 B.C.E. through 200 C.E.) and following.

7. James C. Vanderkamm, *The Dead Sea Scrolls Today* (Grand Rapids: Wm. B. Eerdmans Publishing Co., 1994), 44.

8. The fullest examples of continuous commentaries are fragments of Isaiah, some psalms, Hosea, Micah, Zephaniah, Nahum, and Habakkuk.

9. Geza Vermes, *The Dead Sea Scrolls in English,* 3d ed. (Sheffield: Sheffield Academic Press, 1987), 289.

10. Gary Porton, "Defining Midrash," in *The Study of Ancient Judaism,* ed. Jacob Neusner (New York: KTAV Publishing House, 1981), 1:62.

11. For an overview of scholarly positions on the study of midrash, see Anthony Saldarini, "Reconstructions of Rabbinic Judaism," in *Early Judaism and Its Modern Interpreters,* ed. Robert A. Kraft and George W. E. Nickelsburg (Philadelphia: Fortress Press and Atlanta: Scholars Press, 1986), 437–77.

12. Steven D. Fraade, *From Tradition to Commentary: Torah and Its Interpretation in the Midrash Sifre to Deuteronomy* (Albany: State University of New York Press, 1991), 25.

13. Cited in Gary Porton, *Understanding Rabbinic Midrash: Text and Commentary* (Hoboken, N.J.: KTAV Publishing House, 1985), 81.

14. For bibliography on this vast discussion, see E. Earle Ellis, *The Old Testament in Early Christianity* (Tübingen: J. C. B. Mohr, 1991), 77–121. For an attractive proposal, see Richard B. Hays, *Echoes of Scripture in the Letters of Paul* (New Haven, Conn.: Yale University Press, 1989). The phenomena of New Testament texts echoing Old Testament texts can be found in virtually all New Testament literature.

15. For biblical interpretation in the early church beyond the canon, see Robert M. Grant and David Tracy, *A Short History of the Interpretation of the Bible,* 2d ed., rev. and expanded (Philadelphia: Fortress Press, 1984).

16. Karen Jo Torjesen, *Hermeneutical Procedure and Theological Method in Origen's Exegesis* (New York: Walter De Gruyter, 1986), 41.

17. Ibid.

18. Ibid., 59.

19. Ibid., 63–64.

20. Ibid., 48.

21. Ibid., 130–33.

22. Ibid., 47.

23. Origen, "Homily XXVII on Numbers," in *Origen,* trans. Rowan A. Greer, The Classics of Western Spirituality (New York: Paulist Press, 1979), 259.

24. See, for example, *The Preaching of Chrysostom,* ed. and with an introduction by Jaroslav Pelikan, Preacher's Paperback Library (Philadelphia: Fortress Press, 1967). Chrysostom often preached through the books of the New Testament passage by passage. Frequently he simply embellished the text as it was unfurled.

25. See, for example, *The Preaching of Augustine,* ed. and with an introduction by Jaroslav Pelikan, Preacher's Paperback Library (Philadelphia: Fortress Press, 1973).

26. Fred W. Meuser, *Luther the Preacher* (Minneapolis: Augsburg Publishing House, 1983), 47.

27. Ibid., 49.
28. Ibid., 57–58.
29. Martin Luther, "On Twelfth Sunday after Trinity, 1531" in *Luther's Works: Sermons I,* ed. John W. Doberstein (Philadelphia: Fortress Press, 1959), 51:222–23.
30. John Calvin, *Institutes of the Christian Religion,* ed. John T. McNeill, trans. Ford L. Battles (Philadelphia: Westminster Press, 1960), 2:1016.
31. T. H. L. Parker, *Calvin's Preaching* (Louisville, Ky.: Westminster/John Knox Press, 1992), 35.
32. Ibid., 107.
33. Ronald S. Wallace, "The Preached Word as the Word of God," in *Readings in Calvin's Theology,* ed. Donald K. McKim (Grand Rapids: Baker Book House, 1984), 231–43.
34. Parker, *Calvin's Preaching* 81–82.
35. Ibid., 85–90.
36. Ibid., 132.
37. Ibid., 139.
38. "Specimen Sermon by Calvin on Luke 2:9–14," in T. H. L. Parker, *The Oracles of God* (London: Lutterworth Press, 1947), 148.
39. Ibid., 148–49.
40. Ibid., 149.
41. Clyde E. Fant Jr. and William M. Pinson Jr., *Twenty Centuries of Great Preaching: An Encyclopedia of Preaching* (Waco, Tex.: Word Books, 1971), 8:7–8.
42. G. Campbell Morgan, *The Westminster Pulpit* (Westwood, N.J.: Fleming H. Revell Co., 1954), 1:85.
43. Ibid., 86.
44. Ibid., 87–89.
45. D. Martyn Lloyd-Jones, *Faith on Trial* (Grand Rapids: Wm. B. Eerdmans Publishing Co., 1965), 43.
46. Ibid., 20.
47. Contemporary biblical scholarship stresses the importance of interpreting the parables in their own right and without importing artificial allegorical interpretation. However, recent voices raise the possibility of legitimate allegorical interpretation of the Bible. See Frances Young, *Virtuoso Theology: The Bible and Interpretation* (Cleveland: Pilgrim Press, 1990); and Stanley Hauerwas, *Unleashing the Scriptures: Freeing the Bible from Captivity in America* (Nashville: Abingdon Press, 1993), 40.
48. Lloyd John Ogilvie, *Autobiography of God* (Ventura, Calif.: Regal Books, 1979), 13.
49. Ibid., 15–16.
50. Lowry is a leader in narrative preaching. On this movement, see, for example, John S. McClure, "Narrative and Preaching: Sorting It All Out," *Journal for Preachers* 15, no. 1 (1991): 24–29.
51. Eugene L. Lowry, *How to Preach a Parable: Designs for Narrative Sermons* (Nashville: Abingdon Press, 1989), 38.
52. Dennis M. Willis, "Noah Was a Good Man," in Lowry, *How to Preach a Parable,* 42–49.

53. Ibid., 45–46.
54. Ibid., 47.
55. Ibid., 48.
56. Ibid., 48–49.
57. Edmund A. Steimle, *Are You Looking for God?* (Philadelphia: Fortress Press, 1957), 4.
58. Ibid.
59. James L. Crenshaw, *Trembling at the Threshold of a Biblical Text* (Grand Rapids: Wm. B. Eerdmans Publishing Co., 1994), 55–56.

CHAPTER 3: PREPARING THE VERSE BY VERSE SERMON

1. The most extensive discussion of feedforward process is John S. McClure, *The Roundtable Pulpit: Where Leadership and Preaching Meet* (Nashville: Abingdon Press, 1995).
2. For fuller discussion of exegetical method, see David L. Bartlett, *Between the Bible and the Church: New Methods for Biblical Preaching* (Nashville: Abingdon Press, 1999); Beverly Roberts Gaventa and Patrick J. Willson, "Preaching as the Re-reading of Scripture," *Interpretation* 52 (1998): 392–406; W. Randolph Tate, *Biblical Interpretation: An Integrated Approach* (Peabody, Mass.: Hendrickson Publishers, 1997); Justo L. Gonzalez and Catherine G. Gonzalez, *The Liberating Pulpit* (Nashville: Abingdon Press, 1994); Thomas G. Long, *Preaching and the Literary Forms of the Bible* (Philadelphia: Fortress Press, 1989); Stephen R. Haynes and Steven L. McKenzie, *To Each Its Own Meaning: An Introduction to Biblical Criticisms* (Louisville, Ky.: Westminster/John Knox Press, 1993); Walter Vogels, *Reaching and Preaching the Bible: A New Semiotic Approach* (Wilmington, Del.: Michael Glazier Publishers, 1986); Ronald J. Allen, *Contemporary Biblical Interpretation for Preaching* (Valley Forge: Judson Press, 1984). Carl R. Holladay and John H. Hayes, *Biblical Exegesis: A Beginner's Handbook*, rev. ed. (Louisville, Ky.: Westminster/John Knox Press, 1983).
3. On such nuanced analysis of historical situation within a text and in the social setting that gave rise to the text, see the luminous work by Stephen Farris, *Preaching That Matters: The Bible and Our Lives* (Louisville, Ky.: Westminster John Knox Press, 1998), especially 75–80.
4. For this understanding of the gospel and this theological method, see Clark M. Williamson and Ronald J. Allen, *A Credible and Timely Word: Process Theology and Preaching* (St. Louis: Chalice Press, 1991), 71–130; idem, *The Teaching Minister* (Louisville, Ky.: Westminster/John Knox Press, 1991), 65–82; idem, *Adventures of the Spirit: A Guide to Worship from the Perspective of Process Theology* (Lanham, Md.: University Press of America, 113–58; idem, *The Vital Church: Teaching, Worship, Community, Service* (St. Louis: Chalice Press, 1998), 25–48; Clark M. Williamson, *A Guest in the House of Israel: Post-Holocaust Theology and the Church* (Louisville, Ky.: Westminster/John Knox Press, 1993), 18–25.
5. David Kelsey, *The Uses of Scripture in Recent Theology* (Philadelphia: Fortress Press, 1975), 172–73.
6. The preeminent work on analogy is Farris, *Preaching That Matters.*

7. On epiphany as a genre, see John J. Collins, *Daniel: With an Introduction to Apocalyptic Literature*, The Forms of the Old Testament Literature (Grand Rapids: Wm. B. Eerdmans Publishing Co., 1984), 8–9.

CHAPTER 4: SUGGESTIONS FOR STRUCTURING THE VERSE BY VERSE SERMON

1. Dan Wakefield, *Going All the Way* (New York: Delacorte Press, 1970), 3.
2. Ibid., 13. Dan Wakefield, *Returning: A Spiritual Journey* (New York: Doubleday, 1988), 3.
3. Ibid., 12.
4. Ibid., 13.
5. Ibid., 20.

CHAPTER 5: TIPS FOR KEEPING THE SERMON INTERESTING

1. Charlotte Lee, *The Oral Reading of the Scriptures* (Boston: Houghton Mifflin, 1974), 23–25.

CHAPTER 6: OCCASIONS FOR PREACHING VERSE BY VERSE

1. For representative approaches, see the introduction.
2. On priestly listening, see Leander Keck, *The Bible in the Pulpit* (Nashville: Abingdon Press, 1978), 61–64.
3. Walter Brueggemann, "The Formfulness of Grief," *Interpretation* 31 (1977): 263–75.
4. For a concise historical summary, see Hughes Oliphant Old, *Worship,* Guides to the Reformed Tradition (Atlanta: John Knox Press, 1984), 57–85.
5. Hughes Oliphant Old, "Preaching by the Book," *Reformed Worship* 8 (1988): 25.
6. Ibid.
7. For critical evaluations of the lectionary, see Ronald J. Allen, "Preaching and the Christian Year," *Handbook of Contemporary Preaching,* ed. Michael Duduit (Nashville: Broadman Press, 1992); 236–46; Eugene L. Lowry, *Living with the Lectionary* (Nashville: Abingdon Press, 1992); Shelly Cochran, *Liturgical Hermeneutics* (Ph.D. diss., Drew University, 1992); David Buttrick, "Preaching the Lectionary: Two Cheers and Some Questions," *Reformed Liturgy and Music* 28, no. 2 (1994): 77–81; Edward Farley, "Preaching the Bible and Preaching the Gospel," *Theology Today* 51 (1994): 90–103.
8. Thomas G. Long, "When the Preacher Is a Teacher," *Journal for Preachers* 16, no. 2 (1993): 24.